God in
American History

The U.S. Capitol
Courtesy National Park Service
Photo by Abbie Rowe

God in
American History

A Documentation of America's Religious Heritage

by

BENJAMIN WEISS

Foreword by Dr. Walter H. Judd

ZONDERVAN PUBLISHING HOUSE

Grand Rapids, Michigan

GOD IN AMERICAN HISTORY

Copyright 1966 by

Benjamin Weiss

First printing ....May, 1966
Second printing ....August, 1966

Library of Congress Catalog Card Number 66-13692

Printed in the United States of America

FOREWORD

Most Americans today enjoy the matchless goodness of living possible for us here without realizing it is largely the material fruit of spiritual roots planted deep in the foundations, structure and institutions of this nation by its founders whose inspiration, motivations and values came from their religious faith, predominantly the Christian faith.

Fruit withers and dies as it loses life-giving contact with its roots. Is it reasonable to expect that the growing lawlessness and secularism of American life can be reversed, or even checked, except as more and more people become aware of and cultivate afresh our nation's spiritual roots? How and where are we to find them?

Benjamin S. Weiss has made a comprehensive and scholarly study of this question. In one volume, *God in American History,* he has assembled the compacts and constitutions, the resolutions, declarations and statements that are the very fabric of our free society. Here one can find quickly not only the interesting historical facts, but their significance — the relation of spiritual cause to material result. The book will be invaluable as a ready reference to the student of both our religious and political heritage. I hope it will be widely read also by all who are concerned to help our nation find its way again. For the difficult trials and temptations of our day in so many ways are basically the same, spiritually, as those through which resolute faith in God and in His unbreakable moral order enabled our forefathers to lead the nation so successfully in their day.

— WALTER H. JUDD
Former Congressman and Christian Statesman

ACKNOWLEDGMENTS

Any statement of appreciation to those who assisted in preparing *God in American History* would be inadequate. The inspiration and help came from many sources. Voices that have long been silent gave information and encouragement to the production of this volume. Librarians gave suggestions to sources of materials unknown to me. Personnel in the Library of Congress and in the Department of Engraving and Printing in Washington gave courteous assistance.

Grateful appreciation is extended to Dr. Irving H. Ahlquist, Dr. Clyde M. Narramore, and Dr. Donald Robertson, whose suggestions and inspiration were of invaluable help.

A word of grateful thanks is offered to Mrs. Marjorie Cook, Mrs. Evelyn Horst, and Mrs. Pauline Lange for assistance in preparing the manuscript.

Loving appreciation is accorded to my wife Unita whose memory was a constant inspiration and help, and to my parents, Andrew and Madeleine Weiss, for their spiritual guidance and for manifesting a deep love and loyalty for their adopted country. Their memory is a continuing benediction.

I humbly thank God for guiding our forefathers to establish this wonderful nation, the United States of America, and permitting me, through the message of this book, to give something of its meaning to oncoming generations.

PREFACE

The purpose of this book is to present documentary evidence that the source of our nation's strength from its beginning has been faith in God as expressed in historic documents and other records. Statesmen, leaders and outstanding citizens have indicated their faith in God through their public and private statements. The nation laid its foundation and developed its political and social structure by its continued adherence to these spiritual and religious ideals.

Churches and Christian institutions in cities, villages, and countryside confirm the deep-seated belief in Jesus Christ and His teachings. Schools, colleges, charitable institutions, hospitals, orphanages, and other institutions are monumental proof of the Christian character of the United States of America.

The true source of our nation's character has been obscured at times by current ideologies and new social theories. Speculation about our historical beginnings and theories about the causes for our growth have inclined to obscure our religious and spiritual ideals. Our forefathers' fortitude, faith, and deep religious convictions in the face of great hardships have almost been forgotten.

Godliness, loyalty, and patriotism are no longer evaluated as sterling values. A new dedication to the great Christian truths and beliefs which spurred our people to build a great nation in a few centuries is needed.

7

A careful examination of the historic documents clearly reveals that our forefathers had deep religious beliefs in God as our Protector and Leader. Numerous documents and records of pronouncements present a continuing expression of their faith in God's guidance and protection from the earliest times to the present date. These statements and writings are included in important official documents of government and official statements by national leaders. They are significant because of the circumstances and situations in which they were given.

Wherever possible the material is presented in chronological order. This provides a framework for a continuing historic record of the religious faith and aspirations of the nation. Faith and trust in Almighty God were expressed not only in times of great national stress and danger, but as an integral part of our national life from the beginning to the present date.

A careful selection of the documents and pronouncements was made to include as much as possible our entire historic background and the ongoing political and social activities. This is by no means an exhaustive record of such statements and documents, but a fair random sampling from many historic situations and occasions. They are presented as unmistakable evidence of our faith in God and in prayer, and in His continuing protection and guidance in our national life and affairs.

INTRODUCTION

The United States of America has reached a high pinnacle of advancement among the nations of the world. This has been achieved in a comparatively short time. History records no other national progress of such dimensions and with such acceleration. Our nation has become the outstanding validation of the soundness of Western Christian culture and civilization.

In this changing world of conflicting ideals and social philosophies the future is never assured. No certified guarantees for a continuing prosperity and progress are in our possession. Our way of life and political system is being challenged in many areas. The price for our freedom is still high and payable in sacrifice and devotion.

The quest for freedom of mind and spirit has assembled within our borders the sons and daughters of many peoples and races. Our nation has become the refuge of those who were willing to give up their homes and friends to come to a new country with better opportunities and freedom of worship and thought. Deep in the hearts of these people was a devotion to a great cause and burning ideals.

Our forefathers came to this continent to find a place where they could worship God unhampered by tradition and religious persecution. In their new home they displayed a devotion to God and to this new way of life which erased every thought of return to the homeland. They built churches where they could worship, as quickly as they built their homes. Schools for the training of their children so that they could learn to read the Bible followed. They wove their spiritual and religious ideals into the very woof of their institutions and government.

In their political and civic life they constantly expressed their reliance on Almighty God for direction and protection. In times of national stress and danger they joined in days of national prayer at the direction of the President. When victory was achieved and there were times of evident prosperity, they responded to a national proclamation by the President for a day of thanksgiving for God's benevolent care.

Each President in his inaugural address expressed his dependence on God for help and guidance during his administration. On many other occasions our Presidents also expressed their belief in God and gave thanks for His benevolent guidance and protection. These occasions are not merely instances of a traditional religious observance, but are evidence of the deep spiritual roots of our people.

The beliefs of the nation are also inscribed on the great public buildings and monuments of the nation. Carved in the stone blocks of the Washington Monument are Bible verses, several presented by groups of school children. Above the speaker's desk of the House of Congress is the inscription, "In God We Trust." This is also the official motto of the United States of

America, instituted by a joint resolution of both Houses of Congress and signed by the President of the United States. On the Tomb of the Unknown Soldier, the symbolic resting place of every soldier who died in the service of his country, and whose grave is unmarked, are the words, "Known only to God."

In a Supreme Court decision one Justice in writing the opinion of the court said, "This is a Christian nation."

We need again to light the backfires of our own devotion to our pledge that we are a *Nation under God*. This is the most unique time of history. Perils and dangers confront within as well as from without. We cannot meet them alone. Our security is still in the God of our fathers. We need to be reminded of our great spiritual heritage and our responsibility to bring these truths to each oncoming generation. This is our sacred responsibility and trust.

IN GOD WE TRUST

12

OFFICIAL MOTTO OF THE UNITED STATES OF AMERICA

"In God We Trust"

On July 3, 1956, President Dwight D. Eisenhower signed a bill which was submitted as a Congressional Resolution making that phrase, "In God We Trust," the national motto of the United States.

Public Law 851, *Chapter* 795, *Joint Resolution, July* 30, 1956:

"Resolved by the Senate and House of Representatives of the United States of America in Congress assembled, That the National Motto of the United States is hereby declared to be, 'In God We Trust.'" Approved July 30, 1956.

On July 11, 1955, a bill was passed by the Senate and House of Representatives to place the inscription, "In God We Trust," on all currency and coins.

Public Law 140, *Chapter* 303, *July* 11, 1955:

To provide that all United States currency shall bear the inscription, "In God We Trust."

Be it enacted by the Senate and House of Representatives of the United States of America in Congress assembled. That at such time as new dies for the printing are adopted in connection with the current program of the Treasury Department to increase the capacity of presses utilized by the Bureau of Engraving and Printing the dies shall bear, at such place or places thereon as the Secretary of the Treasury may determine to be appropriate, the inscription, "In God We Trust," and thereafter this inscription shall appear on all United States currency and coins. Approved July 11, 1955.

CONTENTS

15

16

God in
American History

PART I

FAITH IN GOD
THE ROOTS OF OUR DEMOCRACY

The Birth of a Nation

First Charter of Virginia

The Mayflower Compact

Fundamental Orders of Connecticut

The New England Confederation

Pennsylvania Charter of Privileges

Benjamin Franklin's Address at the Formation of the Constitution

The Declaration of Independence

Virginia Statute of Religious Liberty

THE BIRTH OF A NATION

All nations have a beginning. The birth of a nation is a tremendous occasion. It is related to geography, history, human relations, social progress and innumerable personal interests.

Beginnings of many nations have been obscured in legend, folklore, and mythology. One nation in particular came into existence as the result of a direct fiat of God. God commanded Abram and his family to leave the country where they dwelt and go to a new country and become a new nation.

> "Now the Lord had said unto Abram, Get thee out of thy country, and from thy kindred, and from thy father's house, unto a land that I will shew thee: And I will make of thee a great nation, and I will bless thee, and make thy name great; and thou shalt be a blessing: And the Lord appeared unto Abram, and said, Unto thy seed will I give this land: and there builded he an altar unto the Lord, who appeared unto him" (Genesis 12:1, 2, 7).

> "Neither shall thy name any more be called Abram, but thy name shall be Abraham; for a father of many nations have I made thee" (Genesis 17:5).

To confirm His promise, God commanded that Abram's name be changed to Abraham, meaning "a father of many nations."

The story of Abraham's migration and his experiences with

God is brought to us from ancient times through the Bible record. This is the story of the birth of a nation.

The beginning of our nation, the United States of America, is recorded in the experiences of groups of people who left their homes and country confident that they were being guided by Almighty God to find a new country where they could worship Him in accordance with the dictates of their conscience. One group of devout Christians left their homeland and emigrated to another country, and later on to the newly discovered continent. They braved the long, dangerous voyage across the sea and after a perilous voyage they sighted land. This was their new home.

While still on board the ship, their leaders assembled in the cabin and prepared a compact, which was to be their guide in their new-found home. This document was the historic *Mayflower Compact*.

These hardy pioneers, and many others who followed, cut all ties with their native countries to embark on a new adventure of social, political and religious life. They, too, prepared a document, the *Declaration of Independence*. It declared that they were dependent upon Almighty God for their preservation and their continued existence as a people and a government.

Starting with thirteen colonies they became the United States of America. The tone of this new government in its inception and continuance repeatedly expressed dependence upon the God who brought this nation into being. Again and again they reaffirmed their assurance of His protection and guidance. Their faith is expressed in national documents, statements of Presidents in their inaugural addresses, in the preambles to state constitutions, and chiseled in the stone and marble of monuments and public buildings.

Our Presidents have, to the man, called upon Almighty God to help them meet the awesome responsibility vested in them as President of the United States of America.

The United States of America is truly a nation "under God." We, the citizens, are charged with a serious and unique responsibility to perpetuate this trusting faith in God to oncoming generations.

First Charter of Virginia

GRANTED BY KING JAMES I
1606

I, JAMES, *by the Grace of God, King of* England, Scotland, France, *and* Ireland, *Defender of the Faith, &c. Whereas our loving and well-disposed Subjects . . . have been humble Suitors unto us, that We would vouchsafe unto them our Licence, to make Habitation, Plantation, and to deduce a Colony of sundry of our People into that Part of* America, *commonly called Virginia, and other Parts and Territories in* America, *either appertaining unto us, or which are not now actually possessed by any Christian Prince or People. . . .*

We, greatly commending, and graciously accepting of, their Desires for the Furtherance of so noble a Work, which may, by the Province of Almighty God, hereafter tend to the Glory of his Divine Majesty, in propagating of Christian *Religion to such People, as yet live in Darkness and miserable Ignorance of the true Knowledge and Worship of God, and may in time bring the Infidels and Savages, living in those Parts, to human Civility, and to a settled and quiet Government; Do, by these our Letters Patents, graciously accept of, and agree to, their humble and well-intended Desires. . . .*

FIRST CHARTER OF VIRGINIA

In December of 1606 one hundred and forty-four persons boarded three small sailing vessels, the *Sarah Constant,* the *Goodspeed,* and the *Discovery,* to enter on an adventure that would change their own lives and initiate a new era in the history of the world. A three-month cruise brought them to the shore of Cape Henry in April, 1607. They planted a colony at Jamestown on May 14, 1607.

A charter had been granted by King James, King of England, Scotland, France, and Ireland, to the London and Plymouth Company to colonize certain areas on the American continent. The charter specified that this colony should bring glory to Almighty God and propagate the Christian religion to people who are living in darkness and "ignorance of the true knowledge and worship of God."

These settlers endured great hardships from hunger and disease. Captain John Smith, with two companions, was sent to procure food from the Indians. They were captured and his two companions were killed, but his life was spared by the intervention of Pocahontas, daughter of the chief. Captain John Smith was later chosen as president of the colony's governing council (1608-1609).

The Mayflower Compact

November 11, 1620

In the name of God, Amen. We whose names are underwritten, the loyall subjects of our dread soveraigne Lord, King James, by the grace of God, of Great Britaine, France, and Ireland king, defender of the faith, etc.

Haveing undertaken for the gloire of God, and advancements of the Christian faith, and honour of our king and countrie, a voyage to plant the first colonie in the Northerne parts of Virginia, doe by these presents solemnly and mutualy in the presence of God, and one of another, covenant and combine ourselves togeather into a civil body politick, for our better ordering and preservation and furtherance of the ends aforesaid; and by virtue hearof to enacte, constitute, and frame shuch just and equall lawes, ordinances, acts, constitutions, and offices, from time to time, as shall be thought most meete and convenient for the generall good of the colonie, unto which we promise all due submission and obedience. In witness whereof we have hereunder subscribed our names at Cap-Codd the 11 of November, in the year of the raigne of our soveraigne Lord, King James of England, France, and Ireland the eighteenth, and of Scotland the fiftie fourth. Anno Dom. 1620.

THE MAYFLOWER COMPACT

Fierce storms had driven them far off their course. Their patent from the English Crown was for a colony in Virginia. On a cold November day they approached land and saw an excellent harbor into which they steered their ship. They decided, regardless of not having rights to colonize there, to make this their home.

These were the Pilgrims who had come from their home country, England, to find a new life in the new world. Since they had no rights to form a colony, they met in the cabin of the *Mayflower* and formed a compact based on the principle of the consent of the government. It was signed by the male members of the group. This was the *Mayflower Compact,* dated November 11, 1620.[1] It was the first permanent New England colony — Plymouth Colony.

Governor William Bradford, in writing of this occasion, said: "Being thus arrived in a good harbor and brought safe to land, they fell upon their knees and blessed the God of Heaven who had brought them over the vast and furious ocean, and delivered them from all the perils and miseries thereof, again to set their feet on the firm and stable earth, their proper element.

[1]According to the Old Style calendar, then used by the English, the Mayflower reached Cape Cod Harbor, now Provincetown, Massachusetts, on Saturday, 11 November, 1620, which was the same day as Saturday, November 21, 1620, according to the New Style calendar with which the Pilgrims had become familiar in Holland, and which the English finally adopted in 1752. — George Ernest Bowman, Massachusetts Society of Mayflower Descendants, Boston, Mass., Nov. 21, 1920.

". . . And for the season it was winter, and they that know the winters of that country know them to be sharp and violent and subject to cruel and fierce storms, dangerous to travel to known places, much more to search an unknown coast. Besides, what could they see but a hideous and desolate wilderness, full of wild beasts and wild men? And what multitudes there might be of them they knew not. . . .

"What could sustain them but the Spirit of God and His grace? . . .

". . . when they came ashore they would use their own liberty; for none had power to command them, the patent they had being for Virginia, and not for New England, which belonged to another government, with which the Virginia Company had nothing to do. And partly that such an act by them done (this their condition considered) might be as firm as any patent, and in some respects more sure. . . ."

The *Mayflower Compact* was their mutual, documented, and signed agreement to make this their permanent settlement and to live in accordance with the precepts included in the *Compact*.[1] They chose John Carver, a godly man and well approved amongst them, as their governor for the year.

---

1 Forty-one of the Mayflower passengers signed the *Compact*. They were the only male members eligible to sign. One passenger died on the voyage; seventeen were sons of passengers; one was a nephew of a passenger; five boys were not with their parents, and there were twenty-nine females. The other nine, Governor Bradford said, were two seamen hired to serve for one year. They were not free to sign. Seven others were called servants by Governor Bradford and according to their contracts were not free agents with the right to sign the *Compact*.

Fundamental Orders of Connecticut

1639

Forasmuch as it hath pleased the Allmighty God by the wise disposition of his divyne pruvidence so to Order and dispose of things that we the Inhabitants and Residents of Windsor, Harteford and Wethersfield are now cohabiting and dwelling in and uppon the River on Conectecotte and the Lands thereunto adioyneing; And well knowing where a people are gathered togather the word of God requires that to mayntayne the peace and union of such a people there should be an orderly and decent Government established according to God, to order and dispose of the affayres of the people at all seasons as occation shall require; doe therefore assotiate and coinoyne our selves to be as one Publike State or Commonwelth; and doe, for our selves and our Successors and such as shall be adioyned to us att any tyme hereafter, enter into Combination and Confederation togather, to mayntayne and presearve the liberty and purity of the gospell of our Lord Jesus which we now professe, as also the disciplyne of the Churches, which according to the truth of the said gospell is now practised amongst us; As also in our Civell Affaires to be guided and governed according to such Lawes, Rules, Orders and decrees as shall be made, ordered & decreed . . .

FUNDAMENTAL ORDERS OF CONNECTICUT

The *Fundamental Orders of Connecticut* were drawn up and adopted by free men of Windsor, Wethersfield, and Hartford in January, 1639. This was the first written constitution that created a government.

Rev. Thomas Hooker, with his New Town congregation, settled in the beautiful Connecticut Valley and founded the town of Hartford. They were followed by others from Massachusetts Bay. Representatives of the three communities of Hartford, Windsor and Wethersford assembled at Hartford and prepared the agreement which were the Fundamental orders outlining in detail the function of government. This constitution remained in force until 1818.

Their earnest belief in God and dependence on His aid, and their purpose to maintain the liberty and purity of the Gospel of Jesus Christ, are clearly outlined in their constitution.

The New England Confederation

May 19, 1643

Whereas we all came into these parts of America with one and the same end and aim, namely, to advance the Kingdom of our Lord Jesus Christ and to enjoy the liberties of the Gospel in purity with peace; and whereas in our settling (by a wise providence of God) we are further dispersed upon the sea coasts and rivers than was at first intended, so that we can not according to our desire with convenience communicate in one government and jurisdiction; and whereas we live encompassed with people of several nations and strange languages which hereafter may prove injurious to us or our posterity. And forasmuch as the natives have formerly committed sundry insolence and outrages upon several Plantations of the English and have of late combined themselves against us: and seeing by reason of those sad distractions in England which they have heard of, and by which they know we are hindered from that humble way of seeking advice, or reaping those comfortable fruits of protection, which at other times we might well expect. We therefore do conceive it our bounden duty, without delay to enter into a present Cosociation amongst ourselves, for mutual help and strength in all our future concernments: That, as in nation and religion, so in other respects, we be and continue one according to the tenor and true meaning of the ensuing articles. . . .

THE NEW ENGLAND CONFEDERATION

Life in the early New England colonies was hard and dangerous. The native Indian inhabitants often raided plantations and
caused other outrages. Because of civil wars in England, little
or no protection could be expected from that source.

Delegates from Plymouth, Connecticut, and New Haven met
with delegates of the Bay Colony in Boston in May, 1643, and
agreed on the *Articles of Confederation*. Rhode Island and the
New Hampshire-Maine region were excluded from the Confederation. The purpose of the Confederation was for common
protection.

New Haven, Massachusetts Bay, Plymouth, and Connecticut
united in a league for their common defense. John Winthrop of
Massachusetts was the first president.

Pennsylvania Charter of Privileges

October 28, 1701

KNOW YE THEREFORE, That for the further Well-being and good Government of the said Province, and Territories and in Pursuance of the Rights and Powers before mentioned, I the said William Penn do declare, grant and confirm. . . .

FIRST. Because no People can be truly happy, though under the greatest Enjoyment of Civil Liberties, if abridged of the Freedom of their Consciences, as to their Religious Profession and Worship: And Almighty God being the only Lord of Conscience, Father of Lights and Spirits; and the Author as well as Object of all divine Knowledge, Faith and Worship, who only doth enlighten the Minds, and persuade and convince the Understandings of People, I do hereby grant and declare, That no person or Persons, inhabiting in this province or Territories, who shall confess and acknowledge One Almighty God, the Creator, Upholder and Ruler of the World; and profess him or themselves obliged to live quietly under the Civil Government, shall be in any Case molested or prejudiced, in his or their Person or Estate, because of his or their conscientious Persuasion or Practice, nor be compelled to frequent or maintain any religious Worship, Place or Ministry, contrary to his or their Mind, or to do or suffer any other Act or Thing, contrary to their religious Persuasion.

AND that all Persons who also profess to believe in Jesus Christ, the Saviour of the World, shall be capable (notwithstanding their other Persuasions and Practices in Point of Conscience and Religion) to serve this Government in any Capacity, both legislatively and executively. . . .

PENNSYLVANIA CHARTER OF PRIVILEGES

William Penn inherited from his father, Admiral Penn, a claim against the King, Charles II, which eventually amounted to 16,000 pounds. Penn petitioned for a grant of land in America to establish a colony under Quaker rule. Charles II settled the claim by granting Penn a proprietary charter. In April, 1683, *The Great Charter and Frame* was formed.

In 1684 Penn returned to England. He fell into disfavor with William, King of England. His colony was taken from him and placed under the authority of the Governor of New York.

Later it was restored to Penn. He was not able to return to America until 1689. In the meantime the affairs of the colony became unsatisfactory and disorganized. Penn agreed to the appointment of committees from the council and assembly to draft a new frame of government. The Charter was finally agreed upon October 28, 1701, and remained in force until the Revolution.

BENJAMIN FRANKLIN

The heated debate moved back and forth for more than a month. Members of the Constitutional Convention violently promoted their own local interests and personal ambitions. The members, intently debating every proposition that was advanced, could come to no agreement.

Washington earnestly reasoned with the delegates, "It is probable that no plan we propose will be adopted." He said, "If, to please the people, we offer what we ourselves disapprove, how can we afterward defend our work? Let us raise a standard to which the wise and honest can repair: the event is in the hand of God."

An elderly gentleman slowly rose from his chair at a crucial moment. It was Benjamin Franklin, the elder statesman. He reproved the members of the convention for their neglect of prayer. "God," he said, "governs in the affairs of men."

Following his address, the members of the Convention soon demonstrated a different attitude of willingness to give and take and the *Constitution* began to take form.

BENJAMIN FRANKLIN'S ADDRESS AT THE FORMATION OF THE CONSTITUTION

Mr. President: *The small progress we have made after four or five weeks close attendance and continual reasonings with each other — our different sentiments on almost every question, several of the last producing as many noes as ayes, is methinks a melancholy proof of the imperfection of the human understanding. We indeed seem to feel our own want of political wisdom, since we have been running about in search of it. We have gone back to ancient history for models of government, and examined the different forms of those republics which, having been formed with the seeds of their own dissolution, no longer exist. And we have viewed modern states all round Europe, but find none of their Constitutions suitable to our circumstances.*

In this situation of this Assembly, groping as it were in the dark to find political truth, and scarce able to distinguish it when presented us, how has it happened, Sir, that we have not hitherto once thought of humbly applying to the Father of Lights to illumine our understanding? In the beginning of the contest with Great Britain, when we were sensible of danger we had daily prayer in this room for divine protection. Our prayers, Sir, were heard, and they were graciously answered. All of us who were engaged in the struggle must have observed frequent instances of a superintending Providence in our favor. To that kind Providence we owe this happy opportunity of consulting in peace on the means of establishing our future national felicity. And have we now forgotten that powerful Friend? Or do we imagine that we no longer need His assistance?

I have lived, Sir, a long time, and the longer I live, the more convincing proofs I see of this truth — that God governs in the affairs of men. And if a sparrow cannot fall to the ground without His Notice, is it probable that an empire can rise without His aid?

We have been assured, Sir, in the sacred writings, that "except the Lord build the house they labor in vain that build it." I firmly believe this; and I also believe that without His concurring aid we shall succeed in this political building no better than the builders of Babel. We shall be divided by our little partial local interests; our projects will be confounded; and we ourselves shall become a reproach and by-word down to future ages. And, what is worse, mankind may hereafter, from this unfortunate instance, despair of establishing governments by human wisdom, and leave it to chance, war, and conquest.

I, therefore, beg leave to move that, henceforth, prayers imploring the assistance of Heaven, and its blessings on our deliberations, be held in this assembly every morning we proceed to business, and that one or more of the clergy in this city be requested to officiate in that service.

The Declaration of Independence

By the Thirteen Colonies

1776

When, in the course of human events, it becomes necessary for one people to dissolve the political bands which have connected them with another, and to assume, among the powers of the earth, the separate and equal station to which the laws of nature and of nature's God entitle them, a decent respect to the opinions of mankind requires that they should declare the causes which impel them to the separation.

We hold these truths to be self-evident, that all men are created equal; that they are endowed by their Creator with certain unalienable rights; that among these, are life, liberty, and the pursuit of happiness. . . .

We, therefore, the representatives of the United States of America, in general Congress assembled, appealing to the Supreme Judge of the world for the rectitude of our intentions, do, in the name, and by the authority of the good people of these colonies, solemnly publish and declare that these united colonies are, and of right ought to be, free and independent states. . . .

And, for the support of this declaration, with a firm reliance on the protection of Divine Providence, we mutually pledge to each other our lives, our fortunes, and our sacred honor.

DECLARATION OF INDEPENDENCE

This was a moment of crisis. During the spring of 1776 one colony after another declared its independence. Congress advised each colony to form a government independent of Great Britain.

On June 7, 1776, Richard Henry Lee of Virginia introduced a resolution which stated that the "colonies, are, and of right ought to be, free and independent states." A committee was appointed on June 10 to prepare a *Declaration of Independence*. The committee included Thomas Jefferson, John Adams, Benjamin Franklin, Roger Sherman, and R. R. Livingston. The committee presented its draft on June 28, 1776. On July 2 a resolution declaring independence was approved. On July 4 the *Declaration of Independence* was adopted and signed by John Hancock. It was then sent to the legislatures of the states.

The colonists claimed that the *Declaration of Independence* expressed the dignity and rights to which they were entitled by nature's God, and that they are endowed by their Creator with certain unalienable rights; that among these are "life, liberty, and the pursuit of happiness."

For the support of the *Declaration* they called on the protection of Divine Providence. The signers mutually pledged to each other, "our lives, our fortunes, and our sacred honor."

Virginia Statute of Religious Liberty

January 16, 1786

Well aware that the opinions and belief of men depend not on their own will, but follow involuntarily the evidence proposed to their minds; that Almighty God hath created the mind free, and manifested his supreme will that free it shall remain by making it altogether insusceptible of restraint; that all attempts to influence it by temporal punishments, or burthens, or by civil incapacitations, tend only to beget habits of hypocrisy and meanness, and are a departure from the plan of the holy author of our religion, who being lord both of body and mind, yet chose not to propagate it by coercions on either, as was in His Almighty power to do, but to extend it by its influence on reason alone. . . .

We, the General Assembly of Virginia do enact that no man shall be compelled to frequent or support any religious worship, place of ministry whatsoever, nor shall be enforced, restrained, molested or burthened in his body or goods, nor shall otherwise suffer, on account of his religious opinions or belief; but that all men shall be free to profess, and by argument to maintain, their opinion in matters of religion, and that the same shall in no wise diminish, enlarge or affect their civil capacities.

VIRGINIA STATUTE OF RELIGIOUS LIBERTY

The principle of religious liberty was included in the Declaration of Rights of 1776. The Anglican Church was, however, the established church in Virginia.

In 1777 the liberals succeeded in repealing the statutes requiring church attendance and support of the established church by all citizens. This did not give entire satisfaction.

Thomas Jefferson prepared a bill for absolute religious freedom of equality. He characterized the long struggle for religious freedom as, "the severest contest in which I have ever been engaged." In 1785 this bill passed the House in Jefferson's absence. In January, 1786, it was accepted by the Senate and became law.[1]

Madison wrote, "Thus in Virginia was extinguished forever the ambitions and hopes of making laws for the human mind." Jefferson regarded this as one of his three memorable contributions to history. The bill was translated into French and Italian and drew attention across the civilized world.

[1] See Huszard and Littlefield *Basic American Documents* for complete text.

PART II

The Faith of the Presidents of the United States as
Expressed in their Inaugural Addresses and
Other Statements

FROM

GEORGE WASHINGTON, 1789

TO

LYNDON B. JOHNSON, 1965

George Washington
John Adams
Thomas Jefferson
James Madison
James Monroe
John Quincy Adams
Andrew Jackson
Martin Van Buren
William Henry Harrison
James K. Polk
Zachary Taylor
Franklin Pierce
James Buchanan
Abraham Lincoln
Ulysses S. Grant
Rutherford B. Hayes

James A. Garfield
Grover Cleveland
Benjamin Harrison
Grover Cleveland
William McKinley
Theodore Roosevelt
William Howard Taft
Woodrow Wilson
Warren C. Harding
Calvin Coolidge
Herbert Hoover
Franklin D. Roosevelt
Harry S. Truman
Dwight D. Eisenhower
John F. Kennedy
Lyndon B. Johnson

THE INAUGURAL ADDRESS

Each President, before he takes office, expresses his political and personal beliefs, ideals, and plan of administration for his term of office in his inaugural address. This is one of the most important addresses he makes in his entire career.

On this momentous occasion, it is quite proper for the President to inform the people of the nation about his religious affirmation as well as his political philosophy. Every President, from George Washington to Lyndon B. Johnson, has included in his inaugural address one or more references to his and the nation's dependence upon God. These statements have become the documented and lasting records of the religious expressions of our presidents.

On some occasions, they were spoken in times of great national crises. At other times they projected the aspirations of a people with great hopes for progress and national realization. The Presidents have continually related the national problems and welfare to a God who is interested; a God whose guidance and help brought the nation into existence. Our Presidents firmly express such belief to their people.

Newspapers of the world publish these historical addresses. They are also communicated to the nation and the world by radio and television. In its 87th session, the Congress of the United States authorized publication of the inaugural addresses of the Presidents from George Washington in 1789 to John F. Kennedy in 1961. Significantly, in these addresses reference is always made to our dependence on Almighty God with a sincere request for divine help in meeting the tremendous responsibilities of the presidential office. In themselves, these pertinent, religious expressions are like a continuing statement of the nation's faith in God. Many of the Presidents were deeply religious. Some may have been more courageous in expressing their faith than others, but without exception they acknowledged the great spiritual heritage of the United States of America.

John Tyler, 10th President, Millard Fillmore, 13th President, Andrew Johnson, 17th President, and Chester A. Arthur, 21st President, did not make inaugural addresses. Each was a vice-president who was sworn into office immediately upon the death of the president.

John Tyler succeeded William Henry Harrison, Millard Fillmore succeeded Zachary Taylor, Andrew Johnson succeeded Abraham Lincoln, and Chester A. Arthur succeeded James A. Garfield.

GEORGE WASHINGTON

Term of Office 1789-1797
Political Party . . . . . . Federalist
Religious Affiliation . . . Episcopalian
Education . . . . No college
Birth date . . . . . February 22, 1732

It was the dawn of a new day for the American Colonies. On April 30, 1789, George Washington was inaugurated as the first President of the United States.

George was the son of Augustine Washington, a planter and farmer. He was baptized on April 5, 1732.

William and Mary College licensed him as a surveyor in 1749, at the age of seventeen. Two years later Virginia commissioned him as a Lieutenant Colonel and three years later as Commander in Chief of the Virginia forces opposing the French and Indians.

When the Continental Congress was formed, he was elected as a delegate, and during the following year was elected as Commander in Chief of the Army by the Second Continental Congress. On February 4, 1789, the electoral college elected George Washington as the first President of the United States.

Organizing the new government was a tremendous undertaking. During the first year of his administration, the Department of War and the Department of State were established, the Treasury Department was formed, and the office of the Attorney General was created. The following year, the first session of the Supreme Court was held, and a year later the Bill of Rights was adopted. The first Thanksgiving Proclamation was issued by the President on October 3, 1789.

He served two terms as President. His farewell address was published in the Philadelphia *Daily American Advertiser* on September 17, 1796.

George Washington was a gentleman of lofty ideals and high moral character. He greatly disapproved of swearing. As General of the Army, he issued a general order to the officers and soldiers: "The General is sorry to be informed that the foolish and wicked practice of profane cursing and swearing, heretofore little known in the army, is growing into fashion. He hopes the officers will, by example as well as by influence, endeavor to check it, and that both they and the men will reflect, that we can have little hope of the blessing of heaven on our arms if we insult it by our impiety and folly. Added to this it is a vice so mean and low, without any temptation, that every man of sense and character detests and despises it."

George Washington never attended college but Harvard, Yale, University of Pennsylvania, and Brown College granted him degrees.

FIRST INAUGURAL ADDRESS —

APRIL 30, 1789

. . . It would be peculiarly improper to omit in this first
official act my fervent supplications to that Almighty Being who
rules over the universe, who presides in the councils of nations,
and whose providential aids can supply every human defect,
that His benediction may consecrate to the liberties and happiness of the people of the United States a Government instituted by themselves for these essential purposes, and may
enable every instrument employed in its administration to execute with success the functions alloted to his charge. In tendering this homage to the Great Author of every public and
private good, I assure myself that it expresses your sentiments
not less than my own, nor those of my fellow-citizens at large
less than either. No people can be bound to acknowledge and
adore the Invisible Hand which conducts the affairs of men
more than those of the United States. Every step by which
they have advanced to the character of an independent nation
seems to have been distinguished by some token of providential agency; and in the important revolution, just accomplished
in the system of their united government the tranquil delibera-

tions and voluntary consent of so many distinct communities from which the event has resulted can not be compared with the means by which most governments have been established without some return of pious gratitude, along with an humble anticipation of the future blessings which the past seem to presage. . . .

We ought to be no less persuaded that the propitious smiles of Heaven can never be expected on a nation that disregards the eternal rules of order and right which Heaven itself has ordained. . . .

I shall take my present leave; but not without resorting once more to the benign Parent of the Human Race in humble supplication that, since He has been pleased to favor the American people with opportunities for deliberating in perfect tranquillity, and dispositions for deciding with unparalleled unanimity on a form of government for the security of their union and the advancement of their happiness, so His divine blessing may be equally conspicuous in the enlarged views, the temperate consultations, and the wise measures on which the success of this Government must depend.

AN ADDRESS OF THE SENATE TO
GEORGE WASHINGTON

May 7, 1789

... We feel, sir, the force and acknowledge the justness of the observation that the foundation of our national policy should be laid in private morality.

If individuals be not influenced by moral principles, it is in vain to look for public virtue. . . .

We commend you, sir, to the protection of Almighty God, earnestly beseeching Him long to preserve a life so valuable and dear to the people of the United States, and that your Administration may be prosperous to the nation and glorious to yourself.

The First Thanksgiving Proclamation

By George Washington

A National Thanksgiving. Whereas it is the duty of all nations to acknowledge the providence of Almighty God, to obey His will, to be grateful for His benefits, and humbly implore His protection and favor; and

Whereas both Houses of Congress have, by their joint committee, requested me to recommend to the people of the United States a day of public thanksgiving and prayer, to be observed by acknowledging with grateful hearts the many signal favors of Almighty God, especially by affording them an opportunity peaceably to establish a form of government for their safety and happiness:

Now, therefore, I do recommend and assign Thursday, the 26th day of November next, to be devoted by the people of these States, to the service of that great and glorious Being who is the beneficent author of all the good that was, that is, or that will be. . . .

And also that we may then unite in most humbly offering our prayers and supplications to the great Lord and Ruler of nations, and beseech Him to pardon our national and other transgressions; . . . to protect and guide all sovereigns and nations . . . to promote the knowledge and practice of true religion and virtue, and the increase of science among them and us; and, generally, to grant unto all mankind such a degree of temporal prosperity as He alone knows to be best.

JOHN ADAMS

Term of Office	1797-1801
Political Party	Federalist
Religious Affiliation	Unitarian
Education	Harvard
Birth date	October 19, 1735

The United States was on the threshold of becoming an effective nation when John Adams was elected as the second President. He was the son of John Adams and the eldest in a family of three boys.

Teaching school in Massachusetts was the beginning of his career. Later he was admitted to the bar at Boston. He was a member of the First Continental Congress, one of the committee of five to draft the *Declaration of Independence* and one of its signers.

When a leader for the Colonial Army was needed, Adams proposed the name of George Washington. Adams was elected President in 1796, but Thomas Jefferson defeated him for election to a second term.

He was the only President whose son became a President of the United States.

. . . Relying, however, on the purity of their intentions, the justice of their cause, and the integrity and intelligence of the people, under an overruling Providence which had as signally protected this country from the first, the representatives of this nation, then consisting of little more than half its present number, not only broke to pieces the chains which were forging and the rod of iron that was lifted up, but frankly cut asunder the ties which had bound them, and launched into an ocean of uncertainty. . . .

I feel it to be my duty to add, if a veneration for the religion of a people who profess and call themselves Christians, and a fixed resolution to consider a decent respect for Christianity among the best recommendations for the public service, can enable me in any degree to comply with your wishes, it shall be my strenuous endeavor that this sagacious injunction of the two Houses shall not be without effect.

. . . And may that Being who is supreme over all, the Patron of Order, the Fountain of Justice, and the Protector in all ages of the world of virtuous liberty, continue His blessing upon this nation and its Government and give it all possible success and duration consistent with the ends of His providence.

From a Speech in Favor of
The Declaration of Independence

Sir, before God, I believe the hour is come. My judgment approves this measure, and my whole heart is in it. All that I have, and all that I am, and all that I hope, in this life, I am now ready here to stake upon it; and I leave off as I began, that live or die, survive or perish, I am for the Declaration. It is my living sentiment, and by the blessing of God it shall be my dying sentiment, Independence *now,* and INDEPENDENCE FOR EVER.

FIRST INAUGURAL ADDRESS —
MARCH 4, 1801

. . . enlightened by a benign religion, professed, indeed, and practiced in various forms, yet all of them inculcating honesty, truth, temperance, gratitude, and the love of man; acknowledging and adoring an overruling Providence, which by all its dispensations proves that it delights in the happiness of man here and his greater happiness hereafter — with all these blessings, what more is necessary to make up a happy and a prosperous people?

. . . And may that Infinite Power which rules the destinies of the universe lead our councils to what is best, and give them a favorable issue for your peace and prosperity.

SECOND INAUGURAL ADDRESS —
MARCH 4, 1805

. . . In matters of religion I have considered that its free exercise is placed by the Constitution independent of the powers of the General Government. I have therefore undertaken on no occasion to prescribe the religious exercises suited to it, but have left them, as the Constitution found them, under the direction and discipline of the church or state authorities acknowledged by the several religious societies.

. . . I shall need, too, the favor of that Being in whose hands we are, who led our fathers, as Israel of old, from their native land and planted them in a country flowing with all the necessaries and comforts of life; who has covered our infancy with His providence and our riper years with His wisdom and power, and to whose goodness I ask you to join in supplications with me that He will so enlighten the minds of your servants, guide their councils, and prosper their measures that whatsoever they do shall result in your good, and shall secure to you the peace, friendship, and approbation of all nations.

THOMAS JEFFERSON

Term of Office 1801-1809

Political Party . . Democratic Republican

Religious Affiliation . . No denomination

Education . . . . William and Mary

Birth date . . . . . . April 13, 1743

The third President of the United States, Thomas Jefferson, was the son of Peter Jefferson, a professor, planter, and surveyor. Thomas was the third child in a family of ten.

He attended William and Mary College and following his graduation was admitted to the bar. The profession of law prepared him for his political career in the young nation. One of his greatest services was as chairman of the committee to frame the *Declaration of Independence*. He was also a deputy delegate to the Continental Congress.

He served two terms as Governor of Virginia. During the second term he resigned the governorship to accept the post as Peace Commissioner. This was followed by his appointment as minister to France. When Washington was President, Jefferson served as Secretary of State.

While Jefferson was President, the United States declared war on Tripoli, the Louisiana purchase was consummated, the Lewis and Clark expedition was organized, and the twelfth amendment to the Constitution was ratified.

"My greatest achievement," he said, "was the bill establishing religious freedom in Virginia."

In a Letter to Charles Thomson
Secretary of the Continental Congress

1816

I, too, have made a wee little book from the same materials, which I call the Philosophy of Jesus; it is a paradigma of His doctrines made by cutting the texts out of the book, and arranging them on the pages of a blank book in a certain order of time or subject. A more beautiful or precious morsel of ethics I have never seen; it is a document in proof that I am a real Christian, that is to say, a disciple of the doctrines of Jesus.

From a Letter to John Adams
October 12, 1813

We must reduce our volume to the simple Evangelists, select, even from them, the very words of Jesus . . . There will be found remaining the most sublime and benevolent code of morals which has ever been offered to man. I have performed this operation for my own use, by cutting verse by verse out of the printed book, and arranging the matter which is evidently His.

FIRST INAUGURAL ADDRESS —

MARCH 4, 1809

. . . But the source to which I look or the aids which alone can supply my deficiencies is in the well-tried intelligence and virtue of my fellow-citizens, and in the counsels of those representing them in the other departments associated in the care of the national interests. In these my confidence will under every difficulty be best placed, next to that which we have all been encouraged to feel in the guardianship and guidance of that Almighty Being whose power regulates the destiny of nations, whose blessings have been so conspicuously dispensed to this rising Republic, and to whom we are bound to address our devout gratitude for the past, as well as our fervent supplications and best hopes for the future.

SECOND INAUGURAL ADDRESS —

MARCH 4, 1813

I should be compelled to shrink if I had less a conviction that the war with a powerful nation, which forms so prominent a feature in our situation, is stamped with that justice which invites the smiles of Heaven on the means of conducting it to a successful termination.

JAMES MADISON

Term of Office 1809-1817

Political Party . . Democratic Republican

Religious Affiliation . . . . Episcopalian

Education . . . . Princeton
(College of New Jersey)

Birth date . . . . . . March 16, 1751

The young nation was going through strenuous times. Serious problems faced the national government when Madison was elected President.

James was the son of James Madison, a justice of the peace and landowner. He was the eldest son of a large family of twelve. Because of ill health his education at Princeton University was interrupted, but he continued his studies at home. Later he returned to Princeton, graduated, and continued a year of graduate studies.

One of his important achievements was drafting the Virginia Guarantee of Religious Liberty. He served as a member of the Continental Congress and as Secretary of State during the administration of Thomas Jefferson. On March 14, 1809, he was inaugurated as President of the United States, and was elected for a second term.

During his administration there were intermittent Indian wars. On June 18, 1812, war was declared against Great Britain, and the British captured Washington on August 25, 1814. The invasion and capture of Washington by the British was a serious experience for the President and his family.

James Madison was the first President who had served as a congressman.

JAMES MONROE

Term of Office 1817-1825

Political Party . . Democratic Republican

Religious Affiliation . . . Episcopalian

Education . . . . . William and Mary

Birth date . . . . . . April 28, 1758

James Monroe was the son of Spence Monroe, a circuit judge and a farmer. James was the eldest of five children.

He attended William and Mary College, but left to join the army, was commissioned as an officer and fought in the battles of White Plains, Brandywine, Germantown, Trenton, and Harlem Heights. General George Washington promoted him to the rank of Captain for bravery under fire at the battle of Trenton.

On his return to civil life, he resumed the study of law in the office of Thomas Jefferson. While in public service he held positions as a member of the Continental Congress, Governor of Virginia, minister to France, minister to negotiate the treaty with England, Secretary of War under James Madison, United States Senator, and President of the United States.

During his administration, Florida was purchased from Spain, and the financial panic of 1819 occurred. The Monroe Doctrine was formulated and proclaimed as a lasting policy against foreign aggression on the continent.

He served two terms as President, and at the close of the second term retired to his farm.

FIRST INAUGURAL ADDRESS —
MARCH 4, 1817

. . . And if we look to the condition of individuals what a proud spectacle does it exhibit! On whom has oppression fallen in any quarter of our Union? What has been deprived of any right of person or property? Who restrained from offering his vows in the mode which he prefers to the Divine Author of his being? It is well known that all these blessings have been enjoyed in their fullest extent.

. . . If we persevere in the career in which we have advanced as far and in the path already traced, we can not fail, under the favor of a gracious Providence, to attain the high destiny which seems to await us.

. . . Relying on the aid to be derived from the other departments of the Government, I enter on the trust to which I have been called by the suffrages of my fellow-citizens with my fervent prayers to the Almighty that He will be graciously pleased to continue to us that protection which He has already so conspicuously displayed in our favor.

SECOND INAUGURAL ADDRESS —
MARCH 5, 1821

. . . That these powerful causes exist, and that they are permanent, is my fixed opinion; that they may produce a like accord in all questions touching, however remotely, the liberty, prosperity, and happiness of our country will always be the object of my most fervent prayers to the Supreme Author of all Good. . . .

With full confidence in the continuance of that candor and generous indulgence from my fellow-citizens at large which I have heretofore experienced, and with a firm reliance on the protection of Almighty God, I shall forthwith commence the duties of the high trust to which you have called me.

INAUGURAL ADDRESS — MARCH 4, 1825

In compliance with an usage coeval with the existence of our Federal Constitution, and sanctioned by the example of my predecessors in the career upon which I am about to enter, I appear, my fellow-citizens, in your presence and in that of Heaven to bind myself by the solemnities of religious obligation to the faithful performance of the duties alloted to me in the station to which I have been called.

. . . To the guidance of the legislative councils, to the assistance of the executive and subordinate departments, to the friendly cooperation of the respective State governments, to the candid and liberal support of the people so far as it may be deserved by honest industry and zeal, I shall look for whatever success may attend my public services; and knowing that "except the Lord keep the city the watchman waketh but in vain," with fervent supplications for His favor, to His overruling providence I commit with humble but fearless confidence my own fate and future destinies of my country.

JOHN QUINCY ADAMS

Term of Office 1825-1829

Political Party . . Democratic Republican

Religious Affiliation . . . . Unitarian

Education . . . . Harvard

Birth date . . . . . . July 11, 1767

A new era was opening for the young nation. The Erie Canal was completed, the first steam locomotive was put into use, and the building of the Baltimore and Ohio Railroad was started. This was the scene when John Quincy Adams was elected President of the United States.

John was the son of a former President, John Adams, and one of a family of five children. He attended Harvard College and later was a member of the faculty as professor of rhetoric and belles lettres. During his father's administration as President he was secretary to the President, minister to the Netherlands, Portugal, Prussia, England, and Russia. While James Monroe was President, John Quincy Adams was Secretary of State.

He was elected President in 1824, but was the unsuccessful candidate for a second term in 1828, afterward serving nine terms as representative to Congress.

John Quincy Adams was the first President who was a member of Phi Beta Kappa.

ANDREW JACKSON

Term of Office 1829-1837

Political Party . . Democratic Republican

Religious Affiliation . . . . Presbyterian

Education . . . . No college

Birth date . . . . . . March 15, 1767

Andrew Jackson was a rugged pioneer personality. Born in a log cabin, he had no opportunity for an education. As a young man he was unable to write his name. The seventh President of the United States, Andrew Jackson was the son of Andrew Jackson, a linen weaver who was born in Ireland.

He studied law, was admitted to the bar, and was elected to the House of Representatives and to the Senate. He was Commander of the Tennessee Militia and served against the Creek Indians. One of his important victories was the defeat of the British in the Battle of New Orleans. In recognition of this achievement, he received the thanks of Congress, and was awarded the Gold Medal by Congressional Resolution.

On March 10, 1821, he was appointed as Governor of Florida. He was the unsuccessful candidate for the presidency against John Quincy Adams, but was elected President of the United States in November, 1828.

An extract of his will was: "First, I bequeath my body to the dust from whence it came and my soul to God, who gave it, hoping for a happy immortality through the atoning merits of our Lord Jesus Christ, the Saviour of the world."

FIRST INAUGURAL ADDRESS —

MARCH 4, 1829

. . . A diffidence, perhaps too just, in my own qualifications will teach me to look with reverence to the examples of public virtue left by my illustrious predecessors, and with veneration to the lights that flow from the mind that founded and the mind that reformed our system. The same diffidence induces me to hope for instruction and aid from the coordinate branches of the Government, and for the indulgence and support of my fellow-citizens generally. And a firm reliance on the goodness of that Power whose providence mercifully protected our national infancy, and has since upheld our liberties in various vicissitudes, encourages me to offer up my ardent supplications that He will continue to make our beloved country the object of His divine care and gracious benediction.

SECOND INAUGURAL ADDRESS —

MARCH 4, 1833

. . . Finally, it is my most fervent prayer to that Almighty Being before whom I now stand, and who has kept us in His hands from the infancy of our Republic to the present day, that He will so overrule all my intentions and actions and inspire the hearts of my fellow-citizens that we may be preserved from dangers of all kinds and continue forever a united and happy people.

INAUGURAL ADDRESS — MARCH 4, 1837

. . . For myself, conscious of but one desire, faithfully to serve my country, I throw myself without fear on its justice and its kindness. Beyond that I only look to the gracious protection of the Divine Being whose strengthening support I humbly solicit, and whom I fervently pray to look down upon us all. May it be among the dispensations of His providence to bless our beloved country with honors and with length of day. May her ways be ways of pleasantness and all her paths be peace!

MARTIN VAN BUREN

Term of Office 1837-1841

Political Party . . . . . . Democratic

Religious Affiliation . . Dutch Reformed

Education . . . . No college

Birth date . . . . . December 5, 1782

Martin Van Buren was the son of Abraham Van Buren, a farmer and innkeeper in New York, and the third child in a family of five.

Martin studied law in New York, and was admitted to the bar. Later he became a counselor of the Supreme Court in New York. During Andrew Jackson's administration, Van Buren was appointed Secretary of State, and was elected Vice President for Jackson's second term.

The Democratic Party nominated Van Buren for President in 1836, and elected him as President of the United States.

During the first year of his administration a serious financial panic occurred. Ten million dollars in notes were authorized to relieve the common distress.

After his first term, he made three unsuccessful attempts to be elected for a second term.

He was the first President born as a citizen of the United States.

WILLIAM HENRY HARRISON

Term of Office 1841

Political Party . . . . Whig

Religious Affiliation . . . Episcopalian

Education . . Hampden - Sidney College

Birth date . . . . . February 9, 1773

The ninth President of the United States, William Henry Harrison, was the son of Benjamin Harrison, a politician and statesman. William was the youngest in a family of seven children.

While he was attending the medical department of the University of Pennsylvania, the Indian War broke out, and he left school to enlist in the army. Later he was promoted to Captain, and became Territorial Governor of Indian Affairs under President John Adams.

A vote of thanks by the Legislatures of Indiana and Kentucky was given him, and he was awarded the Gold Medal from Congress for his victory at the Battle of the Thames.

On March 4, 1828, he was elected to the Senate of the United States from Ohio. He was inaugurated as President on March 4, 1841. During the inauguration ceremonies, he contracted a cold from which he never recovered. He died on April 4, 1841.

INAUGURAL ADDRESS — MARCH 4, 1841

. . . These precious privileges, and those scarcely less important of giving expression to his thoughts and opinions, either by writing or speaking, unrestrained but by the liability for injury to others, and that of a full participation in all the advantages which flow from the Government, the acknowledged property of all, the American citizen derives from no charter granted by his fellow-man. He claims them because he is himself a man, fashioned by the same Almighty hand as the rest of his species and entitled to a full share of the blessings with which He has endowed them. . . .

I deem the present occasion sufficiently important and solemn to justify me in expressing to my fellow-citizens a profound reverence for the Christian religion and a thorough conviction that sound morals, religious liberty, and a just sense of religious responsibility are essentially connected with all true and lasting happiness; and to that Good Being who has blessed us by the gifts of civil and religious freedom, who watched over and prospered the labors of our fathers and has hitherto preserved to us institutions far exceeding in excellence those of any other people, let us unite in fervently commending every interest of our beloved country in all future time.

INAUGURAL ADDRESS — MARCH 4, 1845

. . . In assuming responsibilities so vast I fervently invoke the aid of that Almighty Ruler of the Universe in whose hands are the destinies of nations and of men to guard this Heaven-favored land against the mischiefs which without His guidance might arise from an unwise public policy. With a firm reliance upon the wisdom of Omnipotence to sustain and direct me in the path of duty which I am appointed to pursue, I stand in the presence of this assembled multitude of my countrymen to take upon myself the solemn obligation "to the best of my ability to preserve, protect, and defend the Constitution of the United States."

. . . Confidently relying upon the aid and assistance of the coordinate departments of the Government in conducting our public affairs, I enter upon the discharge of the high duties which have been assigned me by the people, again humbly supplicating that Divine Being who has watched over and protected our beloved country from its infancy to the present hour to continue His gracious benedictions upon us, that we may continue to be a prosperous and happy people.

JAMES KNOX POLK

Term of Office 1845-1849

Political Party . . . . . . Democratic

Religious Affiliation . . . Episcopalian

Education . University of North Carolina

Birth date . . . . . November 2, 1795

It was the beginning of a new era. America was expanding to the westward. Trouble was looming between Mexico and the United States.

James Polk's father, Samuel Polk, was a plantation farmer. James was one of a family of ten children. He graduated from the University of North Carolina, and was admitted to the bar at Columbia, Tennessee. In 1839 he was elected Governor of Tennessee.

81

On his nomination for President on May 29, 1844, the news was sent by telegraph for the first time. He was elected President as the first "Dark Horse" candidate.

President Polk was baptized on June 8, 1849, by Rev. McFerren, a Methodist minister, one week before his death. This was in fulfillment of a promise he had made.

ZACHARY TAYLOR

Term of Office 1849-1850

Political Party . . . . Whig

Religious Affiliation . . . Episcopalian

Education . . . . No college

Birth date . . . . November 24, 1784

The country was deeply involved in Indian wars during the period of Zachary Taylor's life. He was a career soldier, and came from a military family. His father was Lt. Col. Richard Taylor, a soldier and a farmer. Zachary was the third child in a family of nine.

He served in the army during the War of 1812, the Indian wars and the Mexican War, during which time he rose to the rank of Major General. One of his outstanding achievements was the defeat of Santa Anna at the Battle of Buena Vista. In honor of this victory, Congress thanked him for his courage, fortitude, skill, and enterprise.

Zachary Taylor was elected President of the United States in November, 1848. He died in office on July 9, 1850, the second President to die in office.

INAUGURAL ADDRESS — MARCH 5, 1849

... In conclusion I congratulate you, my fellow-citizens, upon the high state of prosperity to which the goodness of Divine Providence has conducted our common country. Let us invoke a continuance of the same protecting care which has led us from small beginnings to the eminence we this day occupy; and let us seek to deserve that continuance by prudence and moderation in our councils, by well-directed attempts to assuage the bitterness which too often marks unavoidable differences of opinion, by the promulgation and practice of just and liberal principles, and by an enlarged patriotism, which shall acknowledge no limits but those of our widespread Republic.

INAUGURAL ADDRESS — MARCH 4, 1853

... It is with an earnest and vital belief that as the Union has been the source, under Providence, of our prosperity to this time, so it is the surest pledge of a continuance of the blessings we have enjoyed, and which we are sacredly bound to transmit undiminished to our children.

... It must be felt that there is no national security but in the nation's humble, acknowledged dependence upon God and His overruling providence.

... I can express no better hope for my country than that the kind Providence which smiled upon our fathers may enable their children to preserve the blessings they have inherited.

PIERCE

FRANKLIN PIERCE

Term of Office 1853-1857

Political Party . . . . . . Democratic

Religious Affiliation . . . . Episcopalian

Education . . . . . Bowdoin College

Birth date . . . . . November 23, 1804

Franklin Pierce was the son of General Benjamin Pierce, a soldier, farmer, and governor. Franklin was the seventh child in a family of eight children. He graduated from Bowdoin College, and later was admitted to the bar. During the Mexican War he enlisted as a private, and later was commissioned as a Brigadier General.

Franklin Pierce was elected President of the United States in November, 1852. He delivered his inaugural address without notes as an oration, instead of reading it as had been the manner of other Presidents.

During his administration Admiral Perry's treaty with Japan was ratified, and the first American flag was flown in Japan.

JAMES BUCHANAN

Term of Office 1857-1861

Political Party . . . . . . Democratic

Religious Affiliation . . . Presbyterian

Education . . . . Dickinson College

Birth date . . . . . . April 23, 1791

The nation was moving steadily toward disaster. The differences between the North and South were growing increasingly more serious when James Buchanan was elected as the fifteenth President.

His father was James Buchanan, a merchant and farmer. James was the second child in a family of eleven. He attended Dickinson College for two years, studied law, and was admitted to the bar. He was elected to the Pennsylvania House of Representatives, and later was appointed minister to Russia. Following this service he was elected to the United States Senate from Pennsylvania. During James Polk's administration, he served as Secretary of State.

James Buchanan was elected President of the United States in November, 1856. He was the only President to remain a bachelor.

INAUGURAL ADDRESS — MARCH 4, 1857

. . . In entering upon this great office I must humbly invoke the God of our fathers for wisdom and firmness to execute its high and responsible duties in such a manner as to restore harmony and ancient friendship among the people of the several states and to preserve our free institutions throughout many generations.

. . . I feel an humble confidence that the kind Providence which inspired our fathers with wisdom to frame the most perfect form of government and union ever devised by man will not suffer it to perish until it shall have been peacefully instrumental by its example in the extension of civil and religious liberty throughout the world.

. . . We ought to cultivate peace, commerce, and friendship with all nations, and this not merely as the best means of promoting our own material interests, but in a spirit of Christian benevolence toward our fellow-men, wherever their lot may be cast.

. . . I shall now proceed to take the oath prescribed by the Constitution, whilst humbly invoking the blessing of Divine Providence on this great people.

Day of Prayer Proclamation

By *Abraham Lincoln*

April 30, 1863

(During the dark age of the Civil War the president, in response to a resolution of the Senate, set apart a day for national prayer and humiliation. President Lincoln designated April 30, 1863, as this day for national prayer. The following is the opening statement of his proclamation):

Whereas the Senate of the United States, devoutly recognizing the Supreme Authority and just government of Almighty God in all the affairs of men and nations, has, by a resolution, requested the President to designate and set apart a day for national prayer and humiliation; and whereas it is the duty of nations, as well as of men, to own their dependence upon the overruling power of God, to confess their sins and transgressions in humble sorrow, yet with assured hope, that genuine repentance will lead to mercy and pardon, and to recognize the sublime truth announced in the Holy Scriptures, and proven by all history, that these nations only are blessed whose God is the Lord. . . .

ABRAHAM LINCOLN

Term of Office 1861-1865

Political Party . . . . . . Republican

Religious Affiliation . . No denomination

Education . . . . No college

Birth date . . . . . February 12, 1809

It was a time of national crisis when Abraham Lincoln became President of the United States. He was the son of a farmer-carpenter from Kentucky and one of four children. There was little opportunity for education other than what he himself acquired.

Abraham worked at odd jobs and as a clerk in a store. Later he studied law, and was admitted to the bar on March 31, 1837.

In 1832 when the Indian wars began, he enlisted as a private. The company immediately elected him as Captain.

Abraham Lincoln was elected President in 1860. The country was deeply stirred by the secession of seven states. One month after his election Virginia, Arkansas, North Carolina, and Tennessee also seceded. He issued the *Emancipation Proclamation* on January 1, 1863, and the thirteenth amendment to the Constitution prohibiting slavery in the United States was passed by Congress after his death. His career came to an abrupt end after the close of the Civil War by the bullet of an assassin on April 14, 1865, at Ford's Theater in Washington, D.C. He died on April 15.

His *Gettysburg Address* is one of the immortal pieces of English literature. He is known as the "Great Emancipator."

FIRST INAUGURAL ADDRESS —

MARCH 4, 1861

. . . Why should there not be a patient confidence in the ulti-
mate justice of the people? Is there any better or equal hope in
the world? In our present differences, is either party without
faith of being in the right? If the Almighty Ruler of Nations,
with His eternal truth and justice, be on your side of the North,
or on yours of the South, that truth and that justice will surely
prevail by the judgment of this great tribunal of the American
people.

. . . Intelligence, patriotism, Christianity, and a firm reliance
on Him who has never yet forsaken this favored land are still
competent to adjust in the best way all our present difficulty.

. . . You have no oath registered in heaven to destroy the government, while I shall have the most solemn one to "preserve,
protect, and defend it."

SECOND INAUGURAL ADDRESS —

MARCH 4, 1865

. . . Neither party expected for the war the magnitude or the
duration which it has already attained. Neither anticipated that
the cause of the conflict itself might cease with or even before
the conflict itself should cease. Each looked for an easier triumph, and a result less fundamental and astounding. Both read

the same Bible and pray to the same God, and each invokes His aid against the other. It may seem strange that any men should dare to ask a just God's assistance in wringing their bread from the sweat of other men's faces, but let us judge not, that we be not judged. The prayers of both could not be answered. That of neither has been answered fully. The Almighty has His own purposes. "Woe unto the world because of offenses; for it must needs be that offenses come, but woe to that man by whom the offense cometh." If we shall suppose that American slavery is one of those offenses which, in the providence of God, must needs come, but which, having continued through His appointed time, He now wills to remove, and that He gives to both North and South this terrible war as the woe due to those by whom the offense came, shall we discern therein any departure from those divine attributes which the believers in a living God always ascribe to Him? Fondly do we hope, fervently do we pray, that this mighty scourge of war may speedily pass away. Yet, if God wills that it continue until all the wealth piled by the bondsman's two hundred and fifty years of unrequited toil shall be sunk, and until every drop of blood drawn with the lash shall be paid by another drawn with the sword, as was said three thousand years ago, so still it must be said, "The judgments of the Lord are true and righteous altogether."

With malice toward none, with charity for all, with firmness in the right as God gives us to see the right, let us strive on to finish the work we are in, to bind up the nation's wounds, to care for him who shall have borne the battle and for his widow and his orphan, to do all which may achieve and cherish a just and lasting peace among ourselves and with all nations.

Letter to Mrs. Bixby

January 21, 1864

Dear Madam,

I have been shown in the files of the War Department a statement of the Adjutant General of Massachusetts that you are the mother of five sons who died gloriously on the field of battle. I feel how weak and fruitless must be any word of mine which should attempt to beguile your grief of a loss so overwhelming, but I cannot refrain from tendering you the consolation that may be found in the thanks of the republic they died to save. I pray that our Heavenly Father may assuage the anguish of your bereavement and leave you only the cherished memories of the loved and lost, and the solemn pride that must be yours to have made so costly a sacrifice upon the altar of freedom.

Yours very sincerely and respectfully,

A. LINCOLN

INAUGURAL ADDRESS — MARCH 4, 1869

. . . In conclusion I ask patient forbearance one toward another throughout the land, and a determined effort on the part of every citizen to do his share toward cementing a happy union; and I ask the prayers of the nation to Almighty God in behalf of this consummation.

ULYSSES S. GRANT

Term of Office 1869-1877
Political Party . . . . . . Republican
Religious Affiliation . . . . Methodist
Education . West Point Military Academy
Birth date . . . . . . April 27, 1822

The nation was slowly recovering from the effects of the Civil War when Ulysses Simpson Grant became the eighteenth President of the United States. His father, Jesse Rool Grant, was a leather tanner and factory manager. Ulysses was the eldest in a family of six children.

He attended the United States Military Academy and was graduated as a Second Lieutenant. During the Mexican War he served as an officer and received the com-

99

mission as Captain. On February 16, 1862, he was commissioned Major General of Volunteers and later Lieutenant General of the United States Army.

General Lee surrendered to General Grant at Appomattox, Virginia. Congress commissioned Grant as General of the Army. President Andrew Johnson appointed him Secretary of War.

In November, 1868, he was elected President and was re-elected for a second term in 1872. After his retirement, he wrote his memoirs, which became a best seller, and brought his family five hundred thousand dollars in royalties after his death.

RUTHERFORD B. HAYES

Term of Office	1877-1881
Political Party	Republican
Religious Affiliation	Methodist
Education	Kenyon College
Birth date	October 4, 1822

The nineteenth President of the United States, Rutherford Birchard Hayes, was the youngest son in a family of five children. His father was Rutherford Hayes, a storekeeper.

Rutherford attended the Methodist Academy at Norwalk, Ohio, and Kenyon College. Later he attended Harvard School of Law, and was admitted to the bar.

He was commissioned a Lieutenant Colonel during the Civil War, and was wounded at the Battle of South Mountain. During the Battle of Cedar Creek, he was severely injured when his horse fell.

Following the close of the war, he was elected Governor of Ohio for two terms. In November, 1876, Rutherford Hayes was elected President of the United States. He declined to be a candidate for a second term.

INAUGURAL ADDRESS — MARCH 5, 1877

. . . Looking for the guidance of that Divine Hand by which the destinies of nations and individuals are shaped, I call upon you, Senators, Representatives, judges, fellow-citizens, here and everywhere, to unite with me in an earnest effort to secure to our country the blessings, not only of material prosperity, but of justice, peace, and union — a union depending not upon the constraint of force, but upon the loving devotion of a free people; "and that all things may be so ordered and settled upon the best and surest foundations that peace and happiness, truth and justice, religion and piety, may be established among us for all generations."

INAUGURAL ADDRESS — MARCH 4, 1881

. . . The emancipated race has already made remarkable progress. With unquestioning devotion to the Union, with a patience and gentleness not born of fear, they have "followed the light as God gave them to see the light." They are rapidly laying the material foundations of self-support, widening their circle of intelligence, and beginning to enjoy the blessings that gather around the homes of the industrious poor. They deserve the generous encouragement of all good men. So far as my authority can lawfully extend they shall enjoy the full and equal protection of the Constitution and the laws.

. . . My countrymen, we do not now differ in our judgment concerning the controversies of past generations, and fifty years hence our children will not be divided in their opinions concerning our controversies. They will surely bless their fathers and their fathers' God that the Union was preserved, that slavery was overthrown, and that both races were made equal before the law. We may hasten or we may retard, but we cannot prevent, the final reconciliation. . . .

The Constitution guarantees absolute religious freedom. Congress is prohibited from making any law respecting an establishment of religion or prohibiting the exercise thereof. . . .

. . . I shall greatly rely upon the wisdom and patriotism of Congress and of those who may share with me the responsibilities and duties of administration, and above all, upon our efforts to promote the welfare of this great people and their Government I reverently invoke the support and blessings of Almighty God.

JAMES ABRAM GARFIELD

Term of Office 1881
Political Party . . . . . . Republican
Religious Affiliation . Disciples of Christ
Education . . . . . Williams College
Birth date . . . . November 19, 1831

James was the son of Abram Garfield, a farmer and canal contractor. He was the fifth child in a family of five. After his father's death he worked on a farm and supported his mother.

His early education consisted of attending the district school three months during the winter. Later he attended Western Reserve Eclectic Institute. After completing his education at Williams College, he taught district school and became professor of ancient languages and literature at Hiram College, Ohio. In 1857 he became head of the Eclectic Institute.

Later he was elected a member of the Ohio State Senate, was admitted to the bar, and during the Civil War was commissioned Lieutenant Colonel of the Ohio Volunteer Infantry. He was promoted to Major General. After the close of the Civil War, he was elected to the House of Representatives and to the Senate. In November, 1880, he was elected President of the United States.

President Garfield was shot in the railroad depot in Washington, D.C., on June 2, 1881, and died on September 19, 1881. He was the fourth President to die in office and the second President to be assassinated.

STEPHEN GROVER CLEVELAND

Term of Office . . 1885-1889; 1893-1897

Political Party . . . . . . Democratic

Religious Affiliation . . . . Presbyterian

Education . . . . No college

Birth date . . . . . . March 18, 1837

Grover Cleveland was the son of Richard Falley Cleveland, a Congregational minister, and was the fifth in a family of nine children.

He worked as a clerk in a store, taught school, served as assistant teacher in the New York Institution for the Blind, served as clerk for a Buffalo, New York, law firm, studied law, and was admitted to the bar. During the following years, he held the office as Assistant District Attorney,

Sheriff of Erie County, New York, and Mayor of Buffalo. He was elected Governor of New York, and in November, 1884, was elected President of the United States. He was defeated in 1888, but was elected for a second term in 1892.

During his administration, the Presidential Succession Act was approved, the American Federation of Labor was organized, Federal Income Tax was declared unconstitutional, the Statue of Liberty was dedicated, and the panic of 1893 occurred.

He was the only President defeated for a second term and later again elected.

FIRST INAUGURAL ADDRESS —
MARCH 4, 1885

. . . And let us not trust to human effort alone, but humbly acknowledge the power and goodness of Almighty God, who presides over the destiny of nations, and who has at all times been revealed in our country's history; let us invoke His aid and His blessings upon our labors.

SECOND INAUGURAL ADDRESS —
MARCH 4, 1893

. . . Deeply moved by the expression of confidence and personal attachment which has called me to this service, I am sure my gratitude can make no better return than the pledge I now give before God and these witnesses of unreserved and complete devotion to the interests and welfare of those who have honored me.

. . . Above all, I know there is a Supreme Being who rules the affairs of men and whose goodness and mercy have always followed the American people, and I know He will not turn from us now if we humbly and reverently seek His powerful aid.

INAUGURAL ADDRESS — MARCH 4, 1889

. . . Entering thus solemnly into covenant with each other, we may reverently invoke and confidently expect the favor and help of Almighty God — that He will give to me wisdom, strength, and fidelity, and to our people a spirit of fraternity and a love of righteousness and peace.

. . . No other people have a government more worthy of their respect and love or a land so magnificent in extent, so pleasant to look upon, and so full of generous suggestion to enterprise and labor. God has placed upon our head a diadem and has laid at our feet power and wealth beyond definition or calculation. But we must not forget that we take these gifts upon the condition that justice and mercy shall hold the reins of power and that the upward avenues of hope shall be free to all the people.

BENJAMIN HARRISON

Term of Office 1889-1893

Political Party . . . . . . Republican

Religious Affiliation . . . . Presbyterian

Education . . . . University of Miami

Birth date . . . . . August 20, 1833

Benjamin Harrison, the twenty-third President of the United States, was the son of John Scott Harrison, a farmer and United States Congressman. Benjamin was the fifth child in a family of thirteen. William Henry Harrison, a former President, was his grandfather.

He attended Miami University, Ohio, was admitted to the bar, practiced law, and was appointed as Reporter of Decisions by the Indiana Supreme Court. On July 14, 1862, he was commissioned as Second Lieutenant in the Indiana Volunteers. Later he was commissioned as Colonel and in 1865 as Brigadier General.

The voters of Indiana elected him to the United States Senate, and in November, 1888, he was elected President of the United States. Grover Cleveland, whom he had defeated for the presidency in 1888, defeated him for a second term.

WILLIAM McKINLEY

Term of Office 1897-1901

Political Party . . . . . . Republican

Religious Affiliation . . . . Methodist

Education . . . . . Allegheny College

Birth date . . . . . . January 29, 1843

William McKinley served as President during the period often referred to as the "Gay Nineties" and the era of American development as a recognized world power. He was the son of William McKinley, an iron manufacturer, the seventh child in a family of nine.

William attended public school and Allegheny College. Following his graduation he taught school near Poland, Ohio. During the Civil War he fought in the battles of

Fishers Hill, Cedar Creek, Conifax Ferry, Antietam, and Opequan. He was commissioned as a Major of volunteers for gallant and meritorious service.

After the close of the war, he studied law and was admitted to the bar. He was elected to the House of Representatives from Ohio and in 1892 was elected Governor of Ohio. In 1896 he was elected President of the United States and was elected for a second term in 1900. The United States engaged in the Spanish American War during his administration.

On September 6, 1901, he was shot by an assassin while attending the Pan-American Exposition at Buffalo, New York. He died on September 14, 1901. His last words were: "It is God's way. His will, not ours, be done."

FIRST INAUGURAL ADDRESS —

MARCH 4, 1897

. . . I assume the arduous and responsible duties of President of the United States, relying upon the support of my countrymen and invoking the guidance of Almighty God. Our faith teaches that there is no safer reliance than upon the God of our fathers, who has so singularly favored the American people in every national trial, and who will not forsake us so long as we obey His commandments and walk humbly in His footsteps.

. . . We may have failed in the discharge of our full duty as citizens of the great Republic, but it is consoling and encouraging to realize that free speech, a free press, free thought, free schools, the free and unmolested right of religious liberty and worship, and free and fair elections are dearer and more universally enjoyed today than ever before. . . .

. . . "I will faithfully execute the office of President of the United States, and will, to the best of my ability, preserve, protect, and defend the Constitution of the United States." This is the obligation I have reverently taken before the Lord Most High. To keep it will be my single purpose, my constant prayer; and I shall confidently rely upon the forbearance and assistance of all the people in the discharge of my solemn responsibilities.

SECOND INAUGURAL ADDRESS —

MARCH 4, 1901

. . . Intrusted by the people for a second time with the office of President, I enter upon its administration appreciating the great responsibilities which attach to this renewed honor and commission, promising unreserved devotion on my part to their faithful discharge and reverently invoking for my guidance the direction and favor of Almighty God. I should shrink from the duties this day assumed if I did not feel that in their performance I should have the co-operation of the wise and patriotic men of all parties. . . .

As heretofore, so hereafter will the nation demonstrate its fitness to administer any new estate which events devolve upon it, and in the fear of God will "take occasion by the hand and make the bounds of freedom wider yet."

THEODORE ROOSEVELT

Term of Office 1901-1909

Political Party . . . . . . Republican

Religious Affiliation . . Dutch Reformed

Education . . . . Harvard

Birth date . . . . . October 27, 1858

Theodore Roosevelt was the son of Theodore Roosevelt, a glass importer and Collector of the Port of New York, and was the second in a family of five children.

Theodore attended public school and graduated from Harvard University. President McKinley appointed him as Assistant Secretary of the Navy, but he resigned to serve in the Spanish American War as a Lieutenant Colonel in command of Roosevelt's Rough Riders.

117

From 1899 to 1901 he served as Governor of New York, was elected Vice President for President McKinley's second term in November, 1900, and succeeded to the office of President when President McKinley was assassinated. In November, 1904, he was elected for a second term.

After he retired from the presidency he engaged in literary pursuits. He was the first president to win the Nobel Peace Prize for effecting a treaty of peace between Russia and Japan at the close of the Russo-Japanese war.

Theodore Roosevelt was the youngest President of the United States to that date. He was referred to as Teddy.

INAUGURAL ADDRESS — MARCH 4, 1905

... My fellow-citizens, no people on earth have more cause to be thankful than ours, and this is said reverently, in no spirit of boastfulness in our own strength, but with gratitude to the Giver of good who has blessed us with the conditions which have enabled us to achieve so large a measure of well-being and of happiness. . . .

We must show, not merely in great crises, but in the everyday affairs of life, the qualities of practical intelligence, of courage, of hardihood, and endurance, and above all the power of devotion to a lofty ideal, which made great the men who founded this Republic in the days of Washington, which made great the men who preserved this Republic in the days of Abraham Lincoln.

INAUGURAL ADDRESS — MARCH 4, 1909

... Having thus reviewed the questions likely to recur during my administration, and having expressed in a summary way the position which I expect to take in recommendations to Congress and in my conduct as an Executive, I invoke the considerate sympathy and support of my fellow-citizens and the aid of the Almighty God in the discharge of my responsible duties.

WILLIAM HOWARD TAFT

Term of Office 1909-1913

Political Party . . . . . . Republican

Religious Affiliation . . . . . Unitarian

Education . . . . Yale

Birth date . . . . . September 15, 1857

William Howard Taft's father, Alphonso Taft, was a lawyer and Secretary of War. William was the seventh in a family of ten children.

He attended Yale University, Cincinnati Law School, and was admitted to the bar on May 8, 1880. This was followed by a judgeship in the Superior Court, Dean of the University of Cincinnati Law School, Governor General of the Philippine Islands, Secretary of War under Theodore Roosevelt, and Provisional Governor of Cuba.

During his administration the Postal Savings Bank was established, parcel post service was instituted, and the sixteenth amendment to the Constitution was ratified, which made it possible to collect income tax. Following his term as President of the United States, he became professor of law at Yale University and Chief Justice of the Supreme Court.

He was the only President who became a Chief Justice of the Supreme Court, and was the first President to be buried in Arlington National Cemetery.

WOODROW WILSON

Term of Office 1913-1921

Political Party . . . . . . Democratic

Religious Affiliation . . . . Presbyterian

Education . . . . Princeton

Birth date . . . . . December 28, 1856

Joseph Ruggles Wilson, the father of Woodrow Wilson, was a Presbyterian minister. Woodrow was the third child in a family of four. He attended Princeton University and University of Virginia Law School. It was necessary for him to discontinue his attendance at law school because of ill health. Later he returned to law school and graduated on June 30, 1881, was admitted to the bar, and practiced law at Atlanta, Georgia.

He received his degree as Doctor of Philosophy from Johns Hopkins University in 1886, taught at Bryn Mawr College, Wesleyan College, and on June 9, 1902, was elected president of Princeton University. Later he was elected Governor of New Jersey, and on November 5, 1912, elected President of the United States. He was elected for a second term in 1916.

During his administration the first World War was fought. He outlined his Fourteen Points to Congress as a basis for world peace. On September 10, 1920, he was awarded the Nobel Prize for Peace.

His political career was spectacular, because in two years and 170 days he rose from a citizen who had never held public office to the presidency of the United States.

FIRST INAUGURAL ADDRESS —
MARCH 4, 1913

. . . And yet it will be no cool process of mere science. The Nation has been deeply stirred, stirred by a solemn passion, stirred by the knowledge of wrong, of ideals lost, of government too often debauched and made an instrument of evil. The feelings with which we face this new age of right and opportunity sweep across our heartstrings like some air out of God's own presence, where justice and mercy are reconciled and the judge and the brother are one. . . .

I summon all honest men, all patriotic, all forward-looking men, to my side. God helping me, I will not fail them, if they will but counsel and sustain me!

SECOND INAUGURAL ADDRESS —
MARCH 5, 1917

. . . We are being forged into a new unity amidst the fires that now blaze throughout the world. In their ardent heat we shall, in God's Providence, let us hope, be purged of faction and division, purified of the errant humors of party and of private interest, and shall stand forth in the days to come with a new dignity of national pride and spirit. Let each man see to it that the dedication is in his own heart, the high purpose of the nation in his own mind, ruler of his own will and desire. . . .

I know now what the task means. I realize to the full the responsibility which it involves. I pray God I may be given the wisdom and the prudence to do my duty in the true spirit of this great people. I am their servant and can succeed only as they sustain and guide me by their confidence and their counsel.

INAUGURAL ADDRESS — MARCH 4, 1921

. . . Standing in this presence, mindful of the solemnity of this occasion, feeling the emotions which no one may know until he senses the great weight of responsibility for himself, I must utter my belief in the divine inspiration of the founding fathers. Surely there must have been God's intent in the making of this new-world Republic. . . .

America is ready to encourage, eager to initiate, anxious to participate in any seemly program likely to lessen the probability of war, and promote that brotherhood of mankind which must be God's highest conception of human relationship. . . .

One cannot stand in this presence and be unmindful of the tremendous responsibility. The world upheaval has added heavily to our tasks. But with the realization comes the surge of high resolve, and there is reassurance in belief in the God-given destiny of our Republic. If I felt that there is to be sole responsibility in the Executive for the America of tomorrow I should shrink from the burden. But here are a hundred millions, with common concern and shared responsibility, answerable to God and country. The Republic summons them to their duty, and I invite co-operation.

I accept my part with single-mindedness of purpose and humility of spirit, and implore the favor and guidance of God in Heaven. With these I am unafraid, and confidently face the future.

I have taken the solemn oath of office on that passage of Holy Writ where in it is asked: "What doth the Lord require of thee but to do justly, and to love mercy, and to walk humbly with thy God?" This I plight to God and country.

WARREN G. HARDING

Term of Office 1921-1923

Political Party . . . . . . Republican

Religious Affiliation . . . . . Baptist

Education . . . . Ohio Central College

Birth date . . . . . November 2, 1865

The "Roaring Twenties" was the expression used for the decade in which Warren Harding served as President. Following the peace treaty at the close of World War I, an era of prosperity came to the United States.

Warren Harding's father, George Tyron Harding, was a newspaper editor. Following his graduation from Ohio Central College, Warren taught school and studied law.

In November, 1884, he with two others purchased the Marion, Ohio, *Star*.

He was elected Lieutenant Governor of Ohio, but was defeated in the election for Governor in 1910. In 1915 he was elected to the Senate from Ohio and in 1920 as President of the United States. The election results were broadcast by radio for the first time.

He died in office on August 2, 1923, the sixth President to die in office.

CALVIN COOLIDGE

Term of Office 1923-1929

Political Party . . . . . . Republican

Religious Affiliation . . Congregationalist

Education . . . . . . Amherst College

Birth date . . . . . . July 4, 1872

Calvin Coolidge's father was John Calvin Coolidge, a farmer, storekeeper, and notary public. Calvin graduated from Amherst College on June 26, 1895. Following his graduation he was admitted to the bar and practiced law at Northhampton, Massachusetts. Later he was elected to the Massachusetts Senate, and then served as Lieutenant Governor and Governor. During President Harding's administration he served as Vice President, and succeeded to the office of President at the death of President Harding. He was elected for a second term in November, 1924. In 1928 he declined to be a candidate for another term.

President Coolidge took his first oath as President at the family homestead at Plymouth, Vermont. His father, a notary public and justice of the peace, administered the oath. The oath was repeated on August 21, 1923, at the Willard Hotel in Washington, D. C.

The Inaugural Address on March 4, 1925, was broadcast by twenty-five radio stations to an audience of more than twenty-five million people. When he was asked if he would be a candidate for a third term, he replied, "I choose not to run."

INAUGURAL ADDRESS — MARCH 4, 1925

. . . If we wish to continue to be distinctively American, we must continue to make that term comprehensive enough to embrace the legitimate desires of a civilized and enlightened people determined in all their relations to pursue a conscientious and religious life. . . .

Here stands its Government, aware of its might but obedient to its conscience. Here it will continue to stand, seeking peace and prosperity, solicitous for the welfare of the wage earner, promoting enterprise, developing waterways and natural resources, attentive to the intuitive counsel of womanhood, encouraging education, desiring the advancement of religion, supporting the cause of justice and honor among the nations. America seeks no earthly empire built on blood and force. No ambition, no temptation, lures her to thought of foreign dominions. The legions which she sends forth are armed, not with the sword, but with the cross. The higher state to which she seeks the allegiance of all mankind is not of human, but of divine origin. She cherishes no purpose save to merit the favor of Almighty God.

INAUGURAL ADDRESS — MARCH 4, 1929

This occasion is not alone the administration of the most sacred oath which can be assumed by an American citizen. It is a dedication and consecration under God to the highest office in service of our people. I assume this trust in the humility of knowledge that only through the guidance of Almighty Providence can I hope to discharge its ever-increasing burdens.

. . . In the presence of my countrymen, mindful of the solemnity of this occasion, knowing what the task means and the responsibility which it involves, I beg your tolerance, your aid, and your cooperation. I ask the help of Almighty God in this service to my country to which you have called me.

HERBERT CLARK HOOVER

Term of Office 1929-1933

Political Party . . . . . . Republican

Religious Affiliation . . Society of Friends

Education . . . . . Stanford University

Birth date . . . . . . August 10, 1874

America was passing through trying experiences during the administration of President Hoover. Panic gripped the stock market on October 29, 1929. The Great Depression was on.

Herbert Hoover's father, Jesse Clark Hoover, was a blacksmith and a farm implement dealer. Herbert's father and mother died before he was ten years old, and he was left an orphan. He was the second in a family of three children.

Hoover worked his way through Stanford University, and graduated in 1895 as a mining engineer. He followed his profession as a consultant in several foreign countries. In 1899 he took his bride to China, and served in the defense of Tientsin during the Boxer outbreak.

In 1914 he began his notable career in relief work by being made Chairman of the American Relief Commission in London and later Chairman of the Belgium Relief Commission. Three years later he was selected to be U.S. Food Administrator and Chairman of the Supreme Economic Conference in Paris. Then followed the chairmanship of the important European Relief Council.

In 1929 he was elected President of the United States, and served for one term. The country was ravaged by the Great Depression during the Hoover administration.

President Truman appointed him as European Food Coordinator in 1946. A year later and in 1953 he was selected as Chairman of the Commission on Organization of the Executive Branch of the United States Government.

The Star Spangled Banner was made the National Anthem by congressional proclamation during his administration.

Hoover was one of the most honored presidents of the United States. Nearly a hundred American and foreign universities and colleges granted him honorary degrees. He was awarded the freedom of more than a dozen cities of the world, and was presented with more than seventy medals and awards.

FRANKLIN DELANO ROOSEVELT

Term of Office 1933-1945

Political Party . . . . . . Democratic

Religious Affiliation . . . . Episcopalian

Education . . . . . Harvard University

Birth date . . . . . January 30, 1882

Franklin Delano Roosevelt was the son of James Roosevelt, a lawyer, financier and vice-president of the Delaware and Hudson Railroad. Franklin attended Harvard University from 1900-1904. He attended Columbia School of Law from 1904-1907 and was admitted to the bar in 1907. Following his admission to the bar he practiced law in New York from 1907-1910. After the close of World War I, he was stricken with infantile paralysis which resulted in a life-long handicap.

Roosevelt was elected Governor of New York in 1929 and President of the United States in 1932, re-elected for a second term in 1936, a third term in 1940, and for a fourth in 1944. He died in office April 12, 1945.

During his administration, the Great Depression afflicted the nation and World War II came to a victorious conclusion for the United States and her allies. In 1933 the Good Neighbor Policy was introduced with Latin America, the Civilian Conservation Corps was originated, the Federal Emergency Relief Act initiated, the Tennessee Valley Authority established, the National Recovery Administration and Public Works Administration were created and the twenty-first amendment of the Constitution, the repeal of prohibition was passed.

Roosevelt was the seventh President of the United States to die in office.

FIRST INAUGURAL ADDRESS —

MARCH 4, 1933

. . . In such a spirit on my part and on yours we face our common difficulties. They concern, thank God, only material things. Values have shrunken to fantastic levels; taxes have risen; our ability to pay has fallen; government of all kinds is faced by serious curtailment of income.

. . . Happiness lies not in the mere possession of money; it lies in the joy of achievement, in the thrill of creative effort.

. . . In this dedication of a Nation we humbly ask the blessing of God. May He protect each and every one of us. May He guide me in the days to come.

SECOND INAUGURAL ADDRESS —

JANUARY 20, 1937

. . . In taking again the oath of office as President of the United States, I assume the solemn obligation of leading the American people forward along the road over which they have chosen to advance.

While this duty rests upon me I shall do my utmost to speak their purpose and to do their will, seeking Divine guidance to help us each and every one to give light to them that sit in darkness and to guide our feet into the way of peace.

THIRD INAUGURAL ADDRESS —

JANUARY 20, 1941

. . . In the face of great perils never before encountered, our strong purpose is to protect and to perpetuate the integrity of democracy.

For this we muster the spirit of America, and the faith of America.

We do not retreat. We are not content to stand still. As Americans, we go forward, in the service of our country, by the will of God.

FOURTH INAUGURAL ADDRESS —

JANUARY 20, 1945

. . . As I stand here today, having taken the solemn oath of office in the presence of my fellow countrymen — in the presence of our God — I know that it is America's purpose that we shall not fail. . . .

The Almighty God has blessed our land in many ways. He has given our people stout hearts and strong arms with which to strike mighty blows for freedom and truth. He has given to our country a faith which has become the hope of all peoples in an anguished world.

So we pray to Him now for the vision to see our way clearly — to see the way that leads to a better life for ourselves and for all our fellow men — to the achievement of His will, to peace on earth.

HARRY S. TRUMAN

Term of Office 1945-1953

Political Party . . . . . . Democratic

Religious Affiliation . . . . . Baptist

Education . . . . No college

Birth date . . . . May 8, 1884

The death of President Roosevelt on April 12, 1945, during World War II moved Vice President Harry S. Truman into the presidency of the United States.

Harry is the son of John Anderson Truman, a farmer. He is the eldest of three children.

During World War I he helped organize the 2nd Missouri Field Artillery, the 129th Field Artillery, and was commissioned First Lieutenant. He served in France as Captain of artillery and participated in four battles. At the close of the war he was discharged with the rank of Major.

On his return to civilian life, he studied law at the Kansas City Law School, was elected judge, United States Senator in 1935, and Vice President in 1944. At the death of President Roosevelt he became President and was elected for a second term in 1948.

During his presidency World War II was won, the atomic bomb was first used in the war with Japan, and the United States engaged in the Korean War.

On November 1, 1950, there was an unsuccessful attempt to assassinate President Truman by two Puerto Rican nationals.

INAUGURAL ADDRESS — JANUARY 20, 1949

. . . In performing the duties of my office, I need the help and prayers of every one of you. I ask for your encouragement and your support. The tasks we face are difficult, and we can accomplish them only if we work together. . . .

We believe that all men are created equal because they are created in the image of God. . . .

These differences between communism and democracy do not concern the United States alone. People everywhere are coming to realize that what is involved is material well-being, human dignity, and the right to believe in and worship God. . . .

But I say to all men, what we have achieved in liberty, we will surpass in greater liberty.

Steadfast in our faith in the Almighty, we will advance toward a world where man's freedom is secure.

To that end we will devote our strength, our resources, and our firmness of resolve. With God's help, the future of mankind will be assured in a world of justice, harmony, and peace.

FIRST INAUGURAL ADDRESS —

JANUARY 20, 1953

Almighty God, as we stand here at this moment my future associates in the executive branch of government join me in beseeching that Thou wilt make full and complete our dedication to the service of the people in this throng, and their fellow citizens everywhere.

Give us, we pray, the power to discern clearly right from wrong, and allow all our words and actions to be governed thereby, and by the laws of this land. Especially we pray that our concern shall be for all the people regardless of station, race, or calling.

May cooperation be permitted and be the mutual aim of those who, under the concepts of our Constitution, hold to differing political faiths; so that all may work for the good of our beloved country and Thy glory. Amen.

. . . The peace we seek, then, is nothing less than the practice and fulfillment of our whole faith among ourselves and in our dealings with others. This signifies more than the stilling of guns, easing the sorrow of war. More than escape from death, it is a way of life. More than a haven for the weary, it is a hope for the brave.

This is the hope that beckons us onward to this century of trial. This is the work that awaits us all, to be done with bravery, with charity, and with prayer to Almighty God.

DWIGHT DAVID EISENHOWER

Term of Office 1953-1961

Political Party . . . . . . Republican

Religious Affiliation . . . . Presbyterian

Education . West Point Military Academy

Birth date . . . . . October 14, 1890

A career soldier was elected as the thirty-fourth President of the United States.

Dwight Eisenhower is the son of David Jacob Eisenhower, a mechanic and business man, and the third in a family of seven sons. In 1915 he graduated from the United States Military Academy, and later attended the Command and General Staff School, the Army War College, and the Army Industrial College.

During World War II, he served as Commanding General European Theatre of Operations, Commander in Chief of Allied Forces in North Africa, directed the invasion of Sicily and Italy, was appointed Supreme Commander of the Allied Expeditionary Forces, and led the D-Day invasion of Europe. On December 20, 1944, he was given the rank of General of the Army. He accepted the surrender of the German army on May 7, 1945.

On February 7, 1948, he retired from active duty in the army, and on June 7, 1948, he was appointed President of Columbia University. He was elected President of the United States on November 4, 1952, and was re-elected for a second term in November, 1956.

President Eisenhower was received into membership of the National Presbyterian Church in Washington, D.C., by baptism and confession of faith on February 1, 1953, and participated as a member of the church in holy communion.

He, with his entire staff, attended a worship service at the National Presbyterian Church, Washington, D.C., on the morning preceding the inauguration service.

After President Eisenhower took the oath of office, and before delivering his inaugural address, he said, "My friends, before I begin the expression of those thoughts I deem appropriate to this moment, would you permit me the privilege of uttering a little private prayer of my own? And I ask you to bow your heads."

SECOND INAUGURAL ADDRESS —

JANUARY 21, 1957

. . . Before all else, we seek, upon common labor as a nation, the blessings of Almighty God. And the hopes in our hearts fashion the deepest prayers of our whole people. . . .

This, nothing less, is the labor to which we are called and our strength dedicated.

And so the prayer of our people carries far beyond our own frontiers, to the wide world of our duty and our destiny.

May the light of freedom, coming to all darkened lands, flame brightly — until at last the darkness is no more.

INAUGURAL ADDRESS — JANUARY 20, 1961

... For I have sworn before you and Almighty God the same solemn oath our forbears prescribed nearly a century and three quarters ago.

The world is very different now. For man holds in his mortal hands the power to abolish all forms of human poverty and all forms of human life. And yet the same revolutionary beliefs for which our forbears fought are still at issue around the globe — the belief that the rights of man come not from the generosity of the state, but from the hand of God. . . .

Now the trumpet summons us again — not as a call to bear arms, though arms we need; not as a call to battle, though embattled we are; but a call to bear the burden of a long twilight struggle, year in, and year out, "rejoicing in hope, patient in tribulation" — a struggle against the common enemies of man: tyranny, poverty, disease, and war itself. . . .

And so, my fellow Americans, ask not what your country can do for you: Ask what you can do for your country.

My fellow citizens of the world: Ask not what America will do for you: Ask what together we can do for the freedom of man.

Finally, whether you are citizens of America or citizens of the world, ask of us the same high standards of strength and sacrifice which we ask of you. With a good conscience our only sure reward, with history the final judge of our deeds, let us go forth to lead the land we love, asking His blessing and His help, but knowing that here on earth God's work must truly be our own.

JOHN FITZGERALD KENNEDY

Term of Office 1961-1963

Political Party . . . . . . Democratic

Religious Affiliation . . Roman Catholic

Education . . . . . Harvard University

Birth date . . . . . . May 29, 1917

John Fitzgerald Kennedy was the son of Joseph Kennedy, a New York financier and Ambassador to Great Britain. John was the second in a family of nine children. He attended Harvard University, worked in the American Embassy in England, served in Congress from 1947 to 1953, and in the Senate from 1953 to 1961. He was elected President in November, 1960.

The period of his administration was a time of serious

international happenings. The cold war continued, the nation was involved in the war of Laos, Russia succeeded in orbiting the first man in space, and the invasion of Pig's Bay, an anti-Castro Cuban revolt, was defeated.

During his administration, he succeeded in having the steel industry retract the steel price raise, recommended the tax cut, which was passed by Congress, and organized the Peace Corps.

He was the youngest President elected to office and the first Roman Catholic President.

The Pulitzer Prize in Biography was awarded to him for his book, *Profiles in Courage,* which became a best seller. *Strategy of Peace* was another book he wrote. It is a collection of his speeches and statements on foreign policy.

The administration of President Kennedy came to a tragic end by an assassin's bullet on November 22, 1963, at Dallas, Texas.

LYNDON B. JOHNSON

Term of Office 1963-

Political Party . . . . . . Democratic

Religious Affiliation . Disciples of Christ

Education . Southwest Texas State Teachers
College

Birth date . . . . . August 27, 1908

Riding in a motorcade through Dallas, Texas, several cars behind President Kennedy, Vice-President Johnson was startled by the sharp crack of a rifle. Almost simultaneously a secret service man sprang on the rear of the car and forced Johnson down into the car.

The assassination of President Kennedy made Lyndon Johnson President of the United States one hour and forty-five minutes after the shot was fired.

149

Lyndon Johnson is the son of Samuel Ely Johnson, a cattleman and public official. His father and mother came from British ancestry. Lyndon is the eldest of five children. He graduated from Southwest Texas State Teachers College at San Marcus, Texas, where he majored in history and social science. Following his graduation he taught public speaking and debate at Houston High School.

He assisted Representative Kleberg in his campaign for United States Congress and accompanied him to Washington as his secretary after the election. While in Washington he attended Georgetown University Law School. President Roosevelt appointed him Texas State Administrator of the newly formed National Youth Administration.

A congressional vacancy in Texas invited Lyndon to enter the campaign for a seat in Congress. He was re-elected to Congress when the United States entered World War II, and was the first Congressman to obtain leave to enter the service. Later, he was appointed President Roosevelt's special emissary to Australia and New Zealand. He was decorated with the Silver Star for gallantry under fire.

In 1948 he was elected to the Senate and became Democratic majority leader. He continued in the Senate until he was elected Vice-President in 1960. He became President of the United States at the assassination of President Kennedy, and was re-elected President by a landslide vote in 1964.

INAUGURAL ADDRESS — JANUARY 20, 1965

My fellow countrymen: On this occasion, the oath I have taken before you and before God, is not mine alone, but ours together. We are one nation and one people. Our fate as a nation and our future as a people rest not upon one citizen but upon all citizens . . .

Our nation's course is abundantly clear. We aspire to nothing that belongs to others. We seek no dominion over our fellow man, but man's dominion over tyranny and misery. . . .

Under this covenant of justice, liberty and union, we have become a nation; prosperous, great and mighty. And we have kept our freedom . . . But we have no promise from God that our greatness will endure. . . .

If we fail now, then we will have forgotten in abundance what we learned in hardships: that democracy rests on faith, that freedom asks more than it gives, and the judgment of God is harshest on those who are most favored . . .

To these trusted public servants and to my family, and those close friends of mine who have followed me down a long winding road, and to all the people of this union and the world — I will repeat today what I said on that sorrowful day in November last year: I will lead and I will do the best I can.

For myself, I ask only in the words of an ancient leader: "Give me now wisdom and knowledge that I may go out and come in before this people: for who can judge this, Thy people, that is so great."

PART III

FAITH IN GOD
IN THE CONSTITUTIONS OF THE STATES

In the Preamble of each state constitution is a statement regarding the faith in God of the people of their state in forming the constitution.

Alabama	Louisiana	Ohio
Alaska	Maine	Oklahoma
Arizona	Maryland	Oregon
Arkansas	Massachusetts	Pennsylvania
California	Michigan	Rhode Island
Colorado	Minnesota	South Carolina
Connecticut	Mississippi	South Dakota
Delaware	Missouri	Tennessee
Florida	Montana	Texas
Georgia	Nebraska	Utah
Hawaii	Nevada	Vermont
Idaho	New Hampshire	Virginia
Illinois	New Jersey	Washington
Indiana	New Mexico	West Virginia
Iowa	New York	Wisconsin
Kansas	North Carolina	Wyoming
Kentucky	North Dakota	

FAITH IN GOD AFFIRMED
IN THE STATES' CONSTITUTIONS

All fifty states of the United States of America have expressed dependence on Almighty God for their preservation and strength. A statement of the faith of the framers of the constitution is included in the preamble, or a reference is made to their faith in God in the body of the constitution of the individual states. The preamble is a statement which explains and gives credence to what is to follow. It becomes the keynote to the entire constitution.

Their dependence on Almighty God was more than an act in extreme emergency or on occasions when the leaders felt they had exhausted their own strength and ability. This great Christian ideal was woven into these constitutions when the leaders of the different commonwealths were in deliberation planning the structure of a state. These statements do not follow a common pattern but are expressions of statesmen in various times and in different geographic areas. They are included as the guideline for the procedure of government in the new state. Together they become the expression of the faith of the people of America.

ALABAMA

Entered the Union December 14, 1819

State Motto — Audemus Jura Nostra Defendere
(We dare to Defend our Rights)

Date of Constitution or Revision — 1901

State Nickname — Cotton State

PREAMBLE

We, the people of the State of Alabama, in order to establish justice, insure domestic tranquillity and secure the blessings of liberty to ourselves and our posterity, invoking the favor and guidance of Almighty God, do ordain and establish the following Constitution and form of government for the State of Alabama.

ALASKA

Entered the Union January 3, 1959

Date of Constitution or Revision — January 3, 1959

State Nickname — Land of the Midnight Sun

Preamble

We, the people of Alaska, grateful to God and to those who founded our nation and pioneered this great land, in order to secure and transmit to succeeding generations our heritage of political, civil, and religious liberty within the Union of States do ordain and establish this constitution for the State of Alaska.

ARIZONA

Entered the Union February 14, 1912

State Motto — Ditat Deus, 1863
(God Enriches)

Date of Constitution or Revision — February 14, 1912

State Nickname — Grand Canyon

PREAMBLE

We, the people of the State of Arizona, grateful to Almighty God for our liberties, do ordain this Constitution.

ARKANSAS

Entered the Union June 15, 1836

State Motto — Regnat Populus, 1864
(The People Rule)

State Nickname — Wonder

Preamble

We, the people of the State of Arkansas, grateful to Almighty God for the privilege of choosing our own form of government, for our civil and religious liberty, and desiring to perpetuate its blessings and secure the same to ourselves and posterity, do ordain and establish this Constitution.

CALIFORNIA

Entered the Union September 9, 1850

State Motto — Eureka

(I Have Found It)

Date of Constitution or Revision — 1879

State Nickname — Golden

PREAMBLE

We, the people of the State of California, grateful to Almighty God for our freedom, in order to secure and perpetuate its blessings, do establish this Constitution.

COLORADO

Entered the Union August 1, 1876

State Motto — Nil sine Numine
(Nothing Without the Deity)

Date of Constitution or Revision — August 1, 1876

State Nickname — Centennial

PREAMBLE

We, the people of Colorado, with profound reverence for the Supreme Ruler of the Universe, in order to form a more independent and perfect government; establish justice; insure tranquillity; provide for the common defense; promote the general welfare and secure the blessings of liberty to ourselves and our posterity; do ordain and establish this Constitution for the "State of Colorado."

CONNECTICUT

Entered the Union January 9, 1788

State Motto — Qui Transtulit Sustinet, 1842
(He Who Transplanted Continues
to Sustain)

Date of Constitution or Revision — 1955

State Nickname — Constitution (Nutmeg)

PREAMBLE

The people of Connecticut, acknowledging with gratitude the good providence of God, in having permitted them to enjoy a free government, do in order more effectually to define, secure, and perpetuate the liberties, rights and privileges which they have derived from their ancestors, hereby, after a careful consideration and revision, ordain and establish the following Constitution and form of civil government.

DELAWARE

Entered the Union December 7, 1787
State Motto — Liberty and Independence
Date of Constitution or Revision — 1847
State Nickname — Diamond (Blue Hen)

PREAMBLE

Through Divine goodness, all men have by nature the rights
of worshipping and serving their Creator according to the
dictates of their consciences, of enjoying and defending life
and liberty, of acquiring and protecting reputation and property, and in general of obtaining objects suitable to their condition, without injury by one to another; and as these rights
are essential to their welfare, for due exercise thereof, power
is inherent in them; and therefore all just authority in the institutions of political society is derived from the people, and
established with their consent, to advance their happiness; and
they may for this end, as circumstances require, from time to
time alter their Constitution of government.

FLORIDA

Entered the Union March 3, 1845

State Motto — In God We Trust, 1846

Date of Constitution or Revision — 1887

State Nickname — Peninsula

PREAMBLE

We, the people of the State of Florida, grateful to Almighty God for our constitutional liberty, in order to secure its blessings and to form a more perfect government, insuring domestic tranquillity, maintaining public order, and guaranteeing equal civil and political rights to all, do ordain and establish this Constitution.

GEORGIA

Entered the Union January 2, 1788
State Motto — Wisdom, Justice, Moderation
Date of Constitution or Revision — 1945
State Nickname — Cracker

PREAMBLE

To perpetuate the principles of free government, insure justice to all, preserve peace, promote the interest and happiness of the citizen, and transmit to posterity the enjoyment of liberty, we, the people of Georgia, relying upon the protection and guidance of Almighty God, do ordain and establish this Constitution.

HAWAII

Entered the Union August 21, 1959

State Motto — Ua Mau Ke Ea O Ka Aina Ika Pono
(The Life of the Land is Perpetuated
in Righteousness)

Date of Constitution or Revision — August 21, 1959

State Nickname — The Aloha State

PREAMBLE

We, the people of the State of Hawaii, grateful for Divine
Guidance, and mindful of our Hawaiian heritage, reaffirm our
belief in a government of the people, by the people, and for
the people, and with an understanding heart toward all of the
people of the earth, do hereby ordain and establish this Constitution for the State of Hawaii.

IDAHO

Entered the Union July 3, 1890

State Motto — Esto Perpetua, 1886
(Mayest Thou Endure Forever!)

Date of Constitution or Revision — January 29, 1890;

Amended — July 3, 1961

State Nickname — Gem

PREAMBLE

We, the people of the State of Idaho, grateful to Almighty God for our freedom, to secure its blessings and promote our common welfare, do establish this Constitution.

ILLINOIS

Entered the Union December 3, 1818

State Motto — State Sovereignty, National Union, 1818

Date of Constitution or Revision — 1870

State Nickname — Prairie (Sucker)

PREAMBLE

We, the people of the State of Illinois — grateful to Almighty God for the civil, political and religious liberty which He hath so long permitted us to enjoy, and looking to Him for a blessing upon our endeavors to secure and transmit the same unimpaired to succeeding generations — in order to form a more perfect government, establish justice, insure domestic tranquillity, provide for the common defense, promote the general welfare, and secure the blessing of liberty to ourselves and our posterity, do ordain and establish this Constitution for the State of Illinois.

INDIANA

Entered the Union December 11, 1816

State Motto — The Crossroads of America

Date of Constitution or Revision — 1851

State Nickname — Hoosier

PREAMBLE

To the end that justice be established, public order maintained, and liberty perpetuated: We, the people of the State of Indiana, grateful to Almighty God for the free exercise of the right to choose our own form of government, do ordain this Constitution.

IOWA

Entered the Union December 28, 1846

State Motto — Our Liberties We Prize and Our Rights
We will Maintain

Date of Constitution or Revision — 1857

State Nickname — Hawkeye

PREAMBLE

We, the people of the State of Iowa, grateful to the Supreme
Being for the blessings hitherto enjoyed, and feeling our dependence on Him for a continuation of these blessings, do
ordain and establish a free and independent government, by
the name of the State of Iowa.

KANSAS

Entered the Union January 29, 1861

State Motto — Ad Astra per Aspera, 1861
(To the Stars Through Difficulties)

Date of Constitution or Revision — January 29, 1861

State Nickname — Sunflower (Jayhawker)

PREAMBLE

We, the people of Kansas, grateful to Almighty God for our civil and religious privileges, in order to insure the full enjoyment of our rights as American citizens, do ordain and establish this Constitution of the State of Kansas.

KENTUCKY

Entered the Union June 1, 1792

State Motto — United We Stand, Divided
We Fall, 1792

Date of Constitution or Revision — 1891

State Nickname — Blue Grass (Corncracker)

PREAMBLE

We, the people of the Commonwealth of Kentucky, grateful
to Almighty God for the civil, political and religious liberties
we enjoy, and desiring to secure the continuance of these
blessings, do ordain and establish this Constitution.

LOUISIANA

Entered the Union April 30, 1812

State Motto — Union, Justice, and Confidence

Date of Constitution or Revision — 1921

State Nickname — Pelican (Creole)

PREAMBLE

We, the people of the State of Louisiana, grateful to Almighty God for the civil, political and religious liberties we enjoy, and desiring to secure the continuance of these blessings, do ordain and establish this Constitution.

MAINE

Entered the Union March 15, 1820

State Motto — Dirigo (I Guide)

Date of Constitution or Revision — March 3, 1820;

Amended, 1876; Recodified, 1953

State Nickname — Pine-Tree

PREAMBLE

(Objects of Government)

We, the people of Maine, in order to establish justice, insure tranquillity, provide for our mutual defense, promote our common welfare, and secure to ourselves and our posterity the blessings of liberty, acknowledging with grateful hearts the goodness of the Sovereign Ruler of the Universe in affording us an opportunity, as favorable to the design; and, imploring His aid and direction in its accomplishment, do agree to form ourselves into a free and independent State, by the style and title of the State of Maine, and do ordain and establish the following Constitution for the government of the same.

MARYLAND

Entered the Union April 28, 1788

State Motto — Scuto Bonae Voluntatis Tuae Coronasti Nos
(With the Shield of Thy Good-Will Thou
Hast Covered Us)

Date of Constitution or Revision — 1867

State Nickname — Old-Line

DECLARATION OF RIGHTS

We, the people of the State of Maryland, grateful to Almighty God for our civil and religious liberty, and taking into our serious consideration the best means of establishing a good Constitution in this State for the sure foundation and more permanent security thereof, declare:

MASSACHUSETTS

Entered the Union February 6, 1788

State Motto — Ense Petit Placidam sub Libertate Quietam, 1780

(By the Sword We Seek Peace, but Peace Only Under Liberty)

Date of Constitution or Revision — October 25, 1780;

Rearranged — 1919

State Nickname — Bay (Old Colony)

PREAMBLE

We, therefore, the people of Massachusetts, acknowledging, with grateful hearts, the goodness of the great Legislator of the Universe, in affording us, in the course of His providence, an opportunity, deliberately and peaceably, without fraud, violence, or surprise, of entering into an Original, explicit, and Solemn Compact with each other; and for forming a New Constitution of Civil Government, for Ourselves and Posterity; and devoutly imploring His direction in so interesting a Design, do agree upon, ordain, and establish the following DECLARATION OF RIGHTS, AND FRAME OF GOVERNMENT, as the Constitution of the Commonwealth of Massachusetts.

MICHIGAN

Entered the Union January 26, 1837

State Motto — Si Queris Peninsulam Amoenam
Circumspice, 1835

(If you seek a pleasant Peninsula,
look around you.)

Date of Constitution or Revision — 1963

State Nickname — Wolverine

PREAMBLE

We, the people of the State of Michigan, grateful
to Almighty God for the blessings of freedom, and earnestly
desiring to secure these blessings undiminished to ourselves and our posterity, do ordain and establish this Constitution.

MINNESOTA

Entered the Union May 11, 1858

State Motto — L'etoile du Nord, 1838
(The Star of the North)

Date of Constitution or Revision — 1857

State Nickname — Gopher

PREAMBLE

We, the people of the State of Minnesota, grateful to God for our civil and religious liberty, and desiring to perpetuate its blessings and secure the same to ourselves and our posterity, do ordain and establish this constitution.

MISSISSIPPI

Entered the Union December 10, 1817

State Motto — Virtute et Armis, 1801
(By Valor and Arms)

Date of Constitution or Revision — 1890

State Nickname — Bayou (Magnolia)

PREAMBLE

We, the people of Mississippi in convention assembled, grateful to Almighty God, and invoking his blessing on our work, do ordain and establish this Constitution.

MISSOURI

Entered the Union August 10, 1821

State Motto — Salux Populi Suprema Lex Esto, 1822
(Let the Welfare of the People be the
Supreme Law)

Date of Constitution or Revision — 1945

State Nickname — Show Me

PREAMBLE

We, the people of Missouri, with profound reverence for the Supreme Ruler of the Universe, and grateful for His goodness, do establish this Constitution for the better government of the State.

MONTANA

Entered the Union November 8, 1889

State Motto — Oro y Plata, 1864
(Gold and Silver)

Date of Constitution or Revision — November 8, 1889

State Nickname — Treasure

PREAMBLE

We, the people of Montana, grateful to Almighty God for the blessings of liberty, in order to secure the advantages of a state government, do in accordance with the provisions of the enabling act of congress, approved the twenty-second of February A.D. 1889, ordain and establish this constitution.

NEBRASKA

Entered the Union March 1, 1867

State Motto — Equality Before the Law, 1867

Date of Constitution or Revision — 1875

State Nickname — Corn Husker (Tree Planter)

PREAMBLE

We, the people, grateful to Almighty God for our freedom, do ordain and establish the following declaration of rights and frame of government, as the Constitution of the State of Nebraska.

NEVADA

Entered the Union October 31, 1864

State Motto — All for Our Country, 1866

Date of Constitution or Revision — October 31, 1864

State Nickname — Sagebrush (Silver)

PREAMBLE

We, the people of the State of Nevada, grateful to Almighty God for our freedom, in order to secure its blessings, insure domestic tranquillity, and form a more perfect government, do establish this Constitution.

NEW HAMPSHIRE

Entered the Union June 21, 1788

State Motto — Live Free or Die

Date of Constitution or Revision — 1784

State Nickname — Granite

Article 5. Religious Freedom Recognized

Every individual has a neutral and unalienable right to worship God according to the dictates of his own conscience and reason. And no subject shall be hurt, molested, or restrained in his person, liberty, or estate, for worshipping God in the manner and season most agreeable to the dictates of his own conscience; or for his religious profession, sentiments or persuasion; provided he doth not disturb the public peace or disturb others in their public worship.

NEW JERSEY

Entered the Union December 18, 1787

State Motto — Liberty and Prosperity, 1776

Date of Constitution or Revision — 1947

State Nickname — Garden State

PREAMBLE

We, the people of the State of New Jersey, grateful to Almighty God for the civil and religious liberty which He hath so long permitted us to enjoy, and looking to Him for a blessing upon our endeavors to secure and transmit the same unimpaired to succeeding generations, do ordain and establish this Constitution.

NEW MEXICO

Entered the Union January 6, 1912

State Motto — Crescit Eundo, 1850

(It Grows as it Goes)

Date of Constitution or Revision — January 6, 1912

State Nickname — Sunshine

PREAMBLE

We, the people of New Mexico, grateful to Almighty God for the blessings of liberty, in order to secure the advantages of a State government, do ordain and establish this constitution.

NEW YORK

Entered the Union July 26, 1788

State Motto — Excelsior, 1809
(Higher)

Date of Constitution or Revision — 1895

State Nickname — Empire

PREAMBLE

We, the People of the State of New York, grateful to Almighty God for our Freedom, in order to secure its blessings, DO ESTABLISH THIS CONSTITUTION.

NORTH CAROLINA

Entered the Union November 21, 1789

State Motto — Esse Quam Videri, 1803
(To Be Rather Than to Seem)

Date of Constitution or Revision — 1868

State Nickname — Tar Heel (Turpentine)

PREAMBLE

We, the people of the State of North Carolina, grateful to Almighty God, the Sovereign Ruler of Nations, for the preservation of the American Union and the existence of our civil, political and religious liberties, and acknowledging our dependence upon Him for the continuance of these blessings to us and our posterity, do, for the more certain security thereof and for the better government of this State, ordain and establish this Constitution.

NORTH DAKOTA

Entered the Union November 2, 1889

State Motto — Liberty and Union, Now and Forever,
One and Inseparable

Date of Constitution or Revision — November 2, 1889

State Nickname — Sioux (Flickertail)

Preamble

We, the people of North Dakota, grateful to Almighty God
for the blessings of civil and religious liberty, do ordain and
establish this Constitution.

OHIO

Entered the Union March 1, 1803

State Motto — "With God, All Things Are Possible"

Date of Constitution or Revision — 1851

State Nickname — Buckeye

PREAMBLE

We, the people of the State of Ohio, grateful to Almighty God for our freedom, to secure its blessings and promote our common welfare, do establish this Constitution.

OKLAHOMA

Entered the Union November 16, 1907

State Motto — Labor Ominia Vincit
(Labor Conquers All Things)

Date of Constitution or Revision — November 16, 1907

State Nickname — Sooner

Preamble

Invoking the guidance of Almighty God, in order to secure and perpetuate the blessing of liberty; to secure just and rightful government; to promote our mutual welfare and happiness, we the people of the State of Oklahoma, do ordain and establish this Constitution.

OREGON

Entered the Union February 14, 1859

State Motto — The Union

Date of Constitution or Revision — February 14, 1859

State Nickname — Beaver

PREAMBLE

We, the people of the State of Oregon, to the end that Justice be established, order maintained, and liberty perpetuated, do ordain this Constitution. . . .

Section 2. Freedom of Worship

All men shall be secure in the natural right, to worship Almighty God according to the dictates of their own consciences.

PENNSYLVANIA

Entered the Union December 12, 1787

State Motto — Virtue, Liberty and Independence, 1800

Date of Constitution or Revision — 1874

State Nickname — Keystone

PREAMBLE

We, the people of the Commonwealth of Pennsylvania, grateful to Almighty God for the blessings of civil and religious liberty, and humbly invoking His guidance, do ordain and establish this Constitution.

RHODE ISLAND

Entered the Union May 29, 1790

State Motto — Hope, 1861

Date of Constitution or Revision — 1843

State Nickname — Little Rhody

PREAMBLE

We, the people of the State of Rhode Island and Providence Plantations, grateful to Almighty God for the civil and religious liberty which He hath so long permitted us to enjoy, and looking to Him for a blessing upon our endeavors to secure and to transmit the same unimpaired to succeeding generations do ordain and establish this constitution of Government.

SOUTH CAROLINA

Entered the Union May 23, 1788
State Motto — Animis Opibusque
(Ready in Soul and Resource)
Date of Constitution or Revision — 1895
State Nickname — Palmetto

PREAMBLE

We, the people of South Carolina, in convention assembled, grateful to God for our liberties, do ordain and establish this Constitution for the preservation and perpetuation of the same.

SOUTH DAKOTA

Entered the Union November 2, 1889

State Motto — Under God the People Rule

Date of Constitution or Revision — November 2, 1889

State Nickname — Coyote

PREAMBLE

We, the people of South Dakota, grateful to Almighty God for our civil and religious liberties, in order to form a more perfect and independent government, establish justice, insure tranquillity, provide for the common defense, promote the general welfare and preserve to ourselves and to our posterity the blessings of liberty, do ordain and establish this Constitution for the State of South Dakota.

TENNESSEE

Entered the Union June 1, 1796

State Motto — Agriculture and Commerce, 1797

Date of Constitution or Revision — 1870

State Nickname — Volunteer

PREAMBLE

Sec. 3 — Rights of Worship Free

That all men have a natural and indefeasible right to worship Almighty God according to the dictates of their own conscience; that no man can of right, be compelled to attend, erect or support any place of worship, or to maintain any minister against his consent; that no human authority can, in any case whatever, control or interfere with the rights of conscience; and that no preference shall ever be given, by law, to any religious establishment or mode of worship.

TEXAS

Entered the Union December 29, 1845

State Motto — Friendship, 1930

Date of Constitution or Revision — 1876

State Nickname — Lone Star

PREAMBLE

Humbly invoking the blessings of Almighty God, the people of the State of Texas, do ordain and establish this Constitution.

UTAH

Entered the Union January 4, 1896

State Motto — Industry

Date of Constitution or Revision — January 4, 1896

State Nickname — Beehive

PREAMBLE

Grateful to Almighty God for life and liberty, we, the people of Utah, in order to secure and perpetuate the principles of free government, do ordain and establish this CONSTITUTION.

VERMONT

Entered the Union March 4, 1791

State Motto — Freedom and Unity, 1866

Date of Constitution or Revision — 1793

State Nickname — Green Mountain

PREAMBLE

That all men have a natural and unalienable right to worship Almighty God, according to the dictates of their own consciences and understandings, as in their opinion shall be regulated by the Word of God: and that no man ought to or of right can be compelled to attend any religious worship, or erect or support any place of worship, or maintain any minister contrary to the dictates of his conscience, nor can any man be justly deprived or abridged of any civil right as a citizen, on account of his religious sentiments, or peculiar mode of religious worship; and that no authority can, or ought to be vested in, or assumed by, any power whatever, that shall in any case interfere with, or in any manner control the rights of conscience, in the free exercise of religious worship. Nevertheless, every sect or denomination of Christians ought to observe the sabbath or Lord's day, and keep up some sort of religious worship, which to them shall seem most agreeable to the revealed will of God.

VIRGINIA

Entered the Union June 25, 1788

State Motto — Sic Semper Tyrannis
(Thus Ever to Tyrants)

Date of Constitution or Revision — 1902

State Nickname — Old Dominion

PREAMBLE

Sec. 2. Religious Freedom

That religion or the duty which we owe to our Creator, and the manner of discharging it, can be directed only by reason and conviction, not by force or violence; and, therefore, all men are equally entitled to the free exercise of religion, according to the dictates of conscience; and that it is the mutual duty of all to practice Christian forbearance, love and charity towards each other.

WASHINGTON

Entered the Union November 11, 1889

State Motto — Alki (By and By)

Date of Constitution or Revision — November 11, 1889

State Nickname — Evergreen

PREAMBLE

We, the people of the State of Washington, grateful to the Supreme Ruler of the Universe for our liberties, do ordain this constitution.

WEST VIRGINIA

Entered the Union June 20, 1863

State Motto — Montani Semper Liberi, 1863
(Mountaineers Are Always Free Men)

Date of Constitution or Revision — 1872

State Nickname — Panhandle

PREAMBLE

Since through Divine providence we enjoy the blessings of civil, political and religious liberty, we, the people of West Virginia, in and through the provisons of the Constitution, reaffirm our faith in and constant reliance upon God and seek diligently to promote, preserve and perpetuate good government in the State of West Virginia for the common welfare, freedom and security for ourselves and our posterity.

WISCONSIN

Entered the Union May 29, 1848

State Motto — Forward

Date of Constitution or Revision — May 29, 1848

State Nickname — Badger

PREAMBLE

We, the people of Wisconsin, grateful to Almighty God for our freedom, in order to secure its blessings, form a more perfect government, insure domestic tranquillity and promote the general welfare, do establish this constitution.

WYOMING

Entered the Union July 10, 1890

State Motto — Cedant Arma Togae, 1868
(Let Arms Yield to the Gown)

Date of Constitution or Revision — July 10, 1890

State Nickname — Equality

Preamble

We, the people of the state of Wyoming, grateful to God for our civil, political and religious liberties, and desiring to secure them to ourselves and perpetuate them to our posterity, do ordain and establish this constitution.

PART IV

FAITH IN GOD
INSCRIBED ON THE CAPITAL BUILDINGS
AND MONUMENTS

The Christian Witness on Our National Capital Buildings and
Monuments:

> The Capitol Building
> Inaugurals
> Prayer Room
> National Motto
>
> The Supreme Court Building
>
> The White House
>
> The Library of Congress
>
> The Washington Monument
>
> The Thomas Jefferson Memorial
>
> The Lincoln Memorial
>
> Gettysburg Address
>
> The Tomb of the Unknown Soldier
>
> The Union Station

THE CHRISTIAN WITNESS
ON OUR NATIONAL CAPITAL BUILDINGS
AND MONUMENTS

King Shalmaneser II, king of Assyria in 860 B.C., commissioned one of his artisans to prepare the black obelisk which contained the records of victories in thirty-one military expeditions. This bears indelible evidence of the greatness of his empire and dynamic of his leadership. A number of other such records have been dug from the ruins of great cities and empires.

One nation appears on the scene of history with a new concept of the source of its greatness and achievement. Its monuments have no records of nations or people conquered or victorious campaigns of the destruction of cities and nations. Its monuments are inscribed with the declaration that the greatness of the nation is the result of God's help and guidance.

Gleaned from the records transmitted by the fathers of this nation are inscriptions giving the source of their strength and courage. Our God is responsible for our greatness — not the cleverness and courage of generals nor the diplomacy of statesmen — our strength is from our God.

In the capital of our nation believers in God and our nation's dependence upon Him have also left inscriptions and initiated practices which would perpetuate the leadership and help of Almighty God in the formation of these United States of America.

Carved in the stone of the Washington Monument, on the walls of the Library of Congress, in the stained glass window in the chapel of the Senate Building, on the Lincoln Memorial, and in other places are the testimonies of this nation's leaders, verifying their belief in and dependence upon God. Procedures have also been instituted in the process of national government through which our dependence upon God and our constant supplication for His aid is expressed.

In presidential inaugural addresses, in Supreme Court sessions, in the openings of Senate and Congress sessions, in the Courts and in other governmental procedures the aid of God is sought for the departments of government and our nation in general.

These practices are a constant reminder well expressed in Kipling's lines in the *Recessional*:

> Lord God of hosts be with us yet,
> Lest we forget.

This is a vital element of the Christian heritage in America. As Americans, we need constantly to remind ourselves that it is our responsibility and duty to perpetuate these ideals to oncoming generations.

THE MEMORY OF THE JUST IS BLESSED.
PRESENTED BY
THE CHILDREN OF THE SUNDAY SCHOOLS
OF THE
METHODIST EPISCOPAL CHURCH,
IN THE
CITY OF NEW YORK.
FEBRUARY 22ND 1855.

One of the Carved Stones Placed on the Inside Wall of the
Washington Monument

U.S. Capitol Building

Courtesy National Park Service
Photo by Abbie Rowe

212

THE CAPITOL BUILDING

The Capitol is a symbol of the nation's life and growth. Within its walls the laws of the nation are enacted. The progress and welfare of the nation are reviewed, the inaugurals of the presidents and vice-presidents are performed. Serious considerations take place on which the very life of the nation depends.

The cornerstone of the Capitol building was laid in September, 1793, by President Washington. The first section was occupied in 1800. It has been in constant process of building and enlargement to the present time. It accurately symbolizes the story of the growth of America.

Fifty-eight years after the first cornerstone was laid a manuscript in the handwriting of Daniel Webster was deposited in the cornerstone for the new Senate and House wings. The manuscript concludes with the following paragraph:

If, therefore, it shall hereafter be the will of God that this structure should fall from the base, that its foundations be upturned, and this deposit brought to the eyes of men, be it then known, that, on this day the Union of the United States of America stands firm, that their constitution still exists unimpaired, and with all of its original usefulness and glory; growing every day stronger and stronger in the affection of the great body of the American people, and attracting more and more the admiration of the world. And all here assembled, whether belonging to public life or, to private life, with hearts devotedly thankful to Almighty God for the preservation of the liberty and happiness of the country, unite in sincere and fervent prayers that this deposit, and the walls and arches, the domes and towers, the columns and the entablatures, now to be erected over it, may endure forever.

God save The United States of America, — Daniel Webster, Secretary of State of United States.

INAUGURALS

January 20 of every fourth year is a milestone in our national history. A new president is installed. A new administration is to be established.

The East Portico of the Capitol is the traditional scene of the inaugural ceremonies. It was not until Andrew Jackson's inauguration, however, that the East Portico was used.

The program is scheduled to begin at noon. But all is prologue to the taking of the oath.

Suddenly the audience is silent. The President-elect is at the podium. He places his left hand on a selected page of an open Bible, raises his right hand, and repeats after the Chief Justice this oath:

> I do solemnly swear (or affirm) that I will faithfully execute the office of President of the United States and will to the best of my ability, preserve, protect, and defend the Constitution of the United States.

He then delivers his inaugural address which presumably sets the tone and outlines the plans for the incoming administration.

The Prayer Room in the Capitol Building

THE PRAYER ROOM

The Prayer Room is a unique addition to our Nation's Capitol. In 1954, both the Senate and the House of Representatives approved a concurrent resolution calling for the establishment of "a room with facilities for prayer and meditation for the use of Members of the Senate and House of representatives."

The House committee considering this action was headed by a Democrat, though the Republican Party was the majority party in Congress. A small room was set aside on the west side of the rotunda for this purpose. In this nondenominational chapel, blue is the dominant color; the furnishings are simple but appropriate. On the altar rests an open Bible, and nearby stands our nation's flag. Freshly cut flowers are placed daily in two vases at the base of a stained glass window through which a subdued light reveals the figure of George Washington in earnest prayer. The etched words of the first verse of the sixteenth Psalm appear in the background:

Preserve me, O God; for in Thee do I put my trust.

Near the top of the window, across the center, are the words:

THIS NATION UNDER GOD

217

Photo of National Motto

218

THE NATIONAL MOTTO IN THE HOUSE OF REPRESENTATIVES CHAMBER

The Speaker's rostrum in the House of Representatives Chamber is against the south wall of the Chamber, directly opposite the Vice-President's rostrum in the Senate Chamber.

Behind the rostrum a panel repeats the marble of the pilasters and is flanked by black and gold Italian marble columns, with caps and bases of Alabama white marble. Across the top of this panel is inscribed in letters of gold the national motto, "In God We Trust." In 1962 the House by resolution (H. Res. 740) provided for the placing of the National Motto on the panel. In the center of the panel, directly behind the Speaker's chair, hangs the flag of the United States. On each side of the flag is a decorative bronze fasces surmounted by laurel wreaths, an axe circled by a bundle of rods. The fasces were a badge of authority for Roman magistrates.

Supreme Court Building
Courtesy National Park Service
Photo by Abbie Rowe

220

THE SUPREME COURT BUILDING

The Supreme Court Building, the home of the Supreme Court of the United States of America, was completed in 1935. The Supreme Court first met in New York City in 1790. It moved from New York to Philadelphia in 1791 and then to Washington in 1801. It met in several different buildings in Washington until the completion of the Supreme Court Building in 1935. It is considered the most beautiful building in our Capitol.

Court begins on the first Monday in October and usually ends about the first of June. When in session the Court convenes at 10 A.M. As the black-robed justices enter the chamber, a crier announces the formal opening of the Court. As they take their seats, the crier's voice is raised as he impressively calls:

Oyez, Oyez, Oyez! All persons having business before the Honorable, the Supreme Court of the United States, are admonished to draw near and give their attention, for the Court is now sitting. God save the United States and the Honorable Court.

The White House
Courtesy National Park Service
Photo by Abbie Rowe

THE WHITE HOUSE

The White House, America's Executive Mansion, was the first building constructed in the Nation's capital. Its cornerstone was laid October 13, 1792. The size of the architect's plans drew criticism from Congress whereupon President Washington advised the architect to reduce the size of the plans. President John Adams and his wife, Abigail, became the first occupants.

During President Truman's administration it was discovered that the White House was no longer safe for occupancy. On December 7, 1949, the reconstruction work commenced and continued until its completion on March 27, 1952.

At the west end of the first floor is the State Dining Room. Its former paneling of dark oak has been painted white. A great chandelier hangs from the ceiling. A portrait of Abraham Lincoln is over the mantelpiece. Cut into the marble facing of the fireplace is the famous inscription authored by John Adams, the first President to occupy the White House:

> "I pray Heaven to bestow the best of Blessings on this White House and on all that shall hereafter inhabit it. May none but Honest and Wise men ever rule under this roof."

Library of Congress

Courtesy Department

224

LIBRARY OF CONGRESS

The Library of Congress is considered the largest library in the world. Over 12,075,000 books and pamphlets are housed in the two buildings. There are more than 16,500,000 manuscripts, more than 2,049,000 pieces and volumes of music; also over 584,000 fine prints and approximately 3,024,-000 photographic negatives, prints, and slides are included in the collection. There are newspaper issues, motion pictures, sound recordings, microfilms and other types of material that bring the total to nearly 39,000,000 items.

This deposit includes every religious book copyrighted in the United States, copies of religious magazines and publications and innumerable photos and copies of pictures of Christian themes. It also contains all of the pieces and volumes of music, the Christian song books, and Christian music that has been copyrighted. It is the greatest depository of Christian music and art in the world. The collection of books includes a copy of the Gutenberg Bible and every Bible copyrighted in the United States.

On the walls of the Library of Congress are these Bible verses and quotations:

"The heavens declare the glory of God; and the firmament showeth His handywork." Psalm 19:1

"Wisdom is the principal thing; therefore get wisdom: and with all thy getting, get understanding." Proverbs 4:7

"What doth the Lord require of thee, but to do justly, and to love mercy, and to walk humbly with thy God." Micah 6:8

"One God, one element, and one far-off divine event, to which the whole creation moves."

"Thank God I also am an American."   —Webster

"For a web begun, God sends thread." —Old proverb.

"That this nation under God, shall have a new birth of freedom; that government of the people, by the people, for the people, shall not perish from the earth." —A. Lincoln (The Pavilion of the Seals).

"Nature is the art of God." —Sir Thomas Browne

THE WASHINGTON MONUMENT

The Washington Monument dominates the skyline of the city of Washington. Its marble shaft is a symbol of simplicity and dignity, an appropriate memorial to our first president. It was built from subscriptions and federal appropriations to memorialize George Washington's achievements and unselfish devotion to principle and to country. It shows the esteem and gratitude of the people of the United States to the Father of their country and their undying faith in the principles and causes for which he stood.

This white marble obelisk measures 555 feet 5½ inches in height. Its hollow column is topped by a marble pyramid, an aluminum cap, and 144 platinum-tipped lightning conductors. Inscribed on the cap are these words: "Praise be to God."

Along the stairway which may be used in descending the shaft are 190 carved tribute blocks set in the inner walls. These stones were donated by states, cities, individuals, societies, and foreign powers, as well as by school children. Ten of these are inscribed with the following quotations, most of which are from the Holy Scriptures.

"God and our native land."

"The memory of the just is blessed." Proverbs 10:7

"Search the Scriptures." John 5:39; Acts 17:11

"Holiness to the Lord." Exodus 28:36; 39:30; Zechariah 14:20

"Psalm CXXXIII" (inscribed on the pages of an open Bible)

"Suffer the little children to come unto me and forbid them not; for of such is the kingdom of God." Luke 18:16

"Train up a child in the way he should go: and when he is old, he will not depart from it." Proverbs 22:6

"In God we trust."

"May Heaven to this union continue its beneficence."

"Auspices of Heaven and the precepts of Washington."

"Praise be to God." (Engraved on the metal tip of the monument.)

Washington Monument
Courtesy National Park Service
Photo by Abbie Rowe

Thomas Jefferson Memorial
Courtesy National Park Service
Photo by Abbie Rowe

THOMAS JEFFERSON MEMORIAL

Thomas Jefferson, who hewed the *Declaration of Independence* out of the dreams, aspirations and longings of countless people in the search for freedom, is memorialized to oncoming generations of American citizens by the Thomas Jefferson Memorial in Washington, D. C. The building expresses the architectural preference of America's third president as depicted by his famous home in Monticello.

A bronze statue of Jefferson stands in the center of the inner hall. The memorial is an appropriate tribute to Jefferson's contribution to the founding of the American Republic.

The beliefs and religious convictions of Thomas Jefferson taken from his writings are inscribed on the panels on the walls of the memorial room. Excerpts from these writings are:

> We hold these truths to be self evident: that all men are created equal, that they are endowed by their Creator with certain inalienable rights, among those are life, liberty and the pursuit of happiness. . . .

> With a firm reliance on the protection of Divine Providence, we mutually pledge our lives, our fortunes and our sacred honor.

> Almighty God hath created the mind free. All attempts to punish it by temporal punishments or burthens . . . are a departure from the plan of the Holy Author of our religion. . . .

> God who gave us life gave us liberty. Can the liberties of a nation be secure when we have removed a conviction that these liberties are the gift of God?

Lincoln Memorial
Courtesy National Park Service
Photo by Abbie Rowe

THE LINCOLN MEMORIAL

The Lincoln Memorial is a monument dedicated to the President of the United States of the Civil War period. Chief Justice Taft of the Supreme Court said at the dedication:

"A shrine at which all can worship, an altar upon which the supreme sacrifice was made for liberty; a sacred religious refuge in which those who love country and love God can find inspiration and repose."

The Memorial was dedicated May 30, 1922. "The white marble temple embraces the essence of his character, steeped in tolerance, in the belief that all people shall be free — free to think, free to seek expression, and free to apply themselves to all enterprise."

A colossal statue of Abraham Lincoln is in the place of honor in the central hall. He is seated in a great armchair over the back of which a flag is draped. Above the statue are carved these words:

IN THIS TEMPLE
AS IN THE HEARTS OF THE PEOPLE
FOR WHOM HE SAVED THE UNION
THE MEMORY OF ABRAHAM LINCOLN
IS ENSHRINED FOREVER

Excerpts from his second inaugural address are inscribed on the wall of the north chamber:

. . . Both read the same Bible and pray to the same God, and each invokes His aid against the other. It may seem strange that any men should dare to ask a just God's assistance in wringing their bread from the sweat of other men's faces, but let us judge not, that we be not judged. The prayers of both could not be answered. That of neither has been answered fully. The Almighty has His own purposes. "Woe unto the world because of offenses; for it must needs be that offenses come, but woe to that man by whom the offense cometh" (Matthew 18:7).

THE GETTYSBURG ADDRESS

November 19, 1863

(Lincoln's famous address was given at the dedication of the national cemetery at Gettysburg. It was here that one of the decisive battles of the Civil War had been fought, with both sides suffering heavy losses. The *Gettysburg Address* is inscribed in stone on the south wall within the memorial chamber).

Four score and seven years ago our fathers brought forth on this continent, a new nation, conceived in Liberty, and dedicated to the proposition that all men are created equal.

Now we are engaged in a great civil war, testing whether that nation or any nation so conceived and so dedicated, can long endure. We are met on a great battle-field of that war. We have come to dedicate a portion of that field, as a final resting place for those who gave their lives that that nation might live. It is altogether fitting and proper that we should do this.

But, in a larger sense, we can not dedicate — we can not consecrate — we can not hallow — this ground. The brave men, living and dead, who struggled here, have consecrated it, far above our poor power to add or detract. The world will little note, nor long remember what we say here, but it can never forget what they did here. It is for us the living, rather, to be dedicated here to the unfinished work which they who fought here have thus far so nobly advanced. It is rather for us to be here dedicated to the great task remaining before us — that from these honored dead we take increased devotion to that cause for which they gave the last full measure of devotion — that we here highly resolve that these dead shall not have died in vain — that this nation, under God, shall have a new birth of freedom — and that government of the people, by the people, for the people, shall not perish from the earth.

Tomb of Unknown Soldier
Courtesy National Park Service
U.S. Army Photograph

TOMB OF THE UNKNOWN SOLDIER

The most famous monuments in the Arlington Cemetery memorializing particular wars are the Memorial Amphitheatre and the Tomb of the Unknown Soldier. Against the background of the principal facade of the Amphitheatre is the Tomb of the Unknown Soldier.

In honoring these heroes of three wars, the nation has paid tribute to more than a half million Americans who in three wars have died for their country: 116,563 in World War I; 407,828 in World War II; and 54,246 in Korea.

The Tomb was carved from a single rectangular block of marble, a design striking in simplicity. The front panel is adorned with a composition of three symbolic figures commemorative of the spirit of the Allies: "Victory through Valor Attaining Peace." The rear panel bears the inscription:

HERE RESTS IN HONORED GLORY AN
AMERICAN SOLDIER KNOWN ONLY TO GOD

In 1921, nearly three years after the end of World War I, six American soldiers serving in the occupation forces in Germany were recalled to France to a chapel at Chalons-sur-

Marne. An American officer met the soldiers outside the chapel and said, "Men, it is my task to choose one of you to perform a great and sacred duty."

In his hand the officer held a bouquet of roses. He turned to one of the six soldiers, Sergeant Edward Younger. "In this church," he said, "are four caskets. In them lie the bodies of four nameless American soldiers. Go into the church. Place a rose on one of the caskets. That is all."

Younger told the rest of the story later: "I went into the church and walked past the caskets. I walked around them three times. Suddenly I stopped. It was as though something had pulled me. A voice seemed to say, 'This is a pal of yours.' I placed the rose on the coffin in front of me and went back out into the sunlight. I still remember the awed feeling I had standing there alone."

On May 30, 1958, the bodies of two Americans of World War II and the Korean War were returned to the United States and interred next to the unknown soldier of World War I. Each of these heroes was selected in simple ceremonies outside the continental United States.

Another view of
The Tomb of the Unknown Soldier
Courtesy National Park Service

Union Station, Washington D.C.

Gateway to the Nation

240

UNION STATION
WASHINGTON, D. C.

Students of public and private schools make the trek to the nation's capital annually by thousands. They are accompanied by their teachers as one of the educational projects for the schools of the Eastern part of the United States. Many of them travel by train and arrive at the Union Station in Washington, D. C. Above the arch at the entrance of the Union Station are these inscriptions from the Bible:

"Ye shall know the truth and the truth shall make you free" (John 8:32).

"The desert shall rejoice and blossom like the rose" (Isaiah 35:1).

These inscriptions are placed above the gateway to the nation's capital to remind all those who come that this is the capital of a Christian nation.

PART V

The National Anthem and some poems of the faith
in God of the American people

THE STAR-SPANGLED BANNER

Frances Scott Key

Oh, say, can you see, by the dawn's early light,
  What so proudly we hailed at the twilight's last gleaming?
Whose broad stripes and bright stars, through the perilous fight,
  O'er the ramparts we watched, were so gallantly streaming?
And the rockets' red glare, the bombs bursting in air,
  Gave proof through the night that our flag was still there.
Oh, say, does that star-spangled banner yet wave
  O'er the land of the free, and the home of the brave?

On the shore, dimly seen through the mists of the deep,
  Where the foe's haughty host in dread silence reposes,
What is that which the breeze, o'er the towering steep,
  As it fitfully blows, half conceals, half discloses?
Now it catches the gleam of the morning's first beam,
  In full glory reflected, now shines on the stream:
'Tis the star-spangled banner; oh, long may it wave,
  O'er the land of the free, and the home of the brave.

And where is that band, who so vauntingly swore

    That the havoc of war and the battle's confusion,

A home and a country should leave us no more?

    Their blood has washed out their foul footsteps' pollution;

No refuge could save the hireling and slave

    From the terror of flight or the gloom of the grave.

And the star-spangled banner in triumph does wave

    O'er the land of the free, and the home of the brave.

Oh, thus be it ever when free-men shall stand

    Between their loved homes and the war's desolation;

Blest with vict'ry and peace, may the Heaven-rescued land

    Praise the Power that hath made and preserved us a nation!

Then conquer we must, when our cause it is just;

    And this be our motto: "In God is our trust!"

And the star-spangled banner in triumph shall wave

    O'er the land of the free, and the home of the brave.

MY COUNTRY, 'TIS OF THEE

Samuel F. Smith

My country, 'tis of thee,
  Sweet land of liberty,
Of thee I sing:
  Land where my fathers died,
Land of the pilgrim's pride,
  From every mountain side
Let freedom ring.

My native country, thee,
  Land of the noble, free,
Thy name I love:
  I love thy rocks and rills,
Thy woods and templed hills;
  My heart with rapture thrills,
Like that above.

Let music swell the breeze,
   And ring from all the trees
Sweet freedom's song:
   Let mortal tongues awake;
Let all that breathe partake;
   Let rocks their silence break,
The sound prolong.

Our father's God, to Thee,
   Author of liberty,
To Thee we sing:
   Long may our land be bright
With freedom's holy light;
   Protect us by Thy might,
Great God, our King.

AMERICA, THE BEAUTIFUL

Katherine Lee Bates

O beautiful for spacious skies,
    For amber waves of grain,
For purple mountain majesties
    Above the fruited plain!
America! America!
    God shed His grace on thee,
And crown thy good with brotherhood
    From sea to shining sea!

O beautiful for pilgrim feet,
    Whose stern, impassioned stress
A thoroughfare for freedom beat
    Across the wilderness!
America! America!
    God mend thine every flaw,
Confirm thy soul in self-control,
    Thy liberty in law!

O beautiful for heroes proved
   In liberating strife,
Who more than self their country loved,
   And mercy more than life!
America! America!
   May God thy gold refine
Till all success be nobleness
   And every gain divine!

O beautiful for patriot dream
   That sees beyond the years
Thine alabaster cities gleam,
   Undimmed by human tears!
America! America!
   God shed His grace on thee,
And crown thy good with brotherhood
   From sea to shining sea!

BIBLIOGRAPHY

An extensive bibliography of books related to the subject, "God in American History."

Abrahamson, Shirley S., *Constitutions of the United States, National and State,* (Legislative Drafting Research Fund of Columbia University), 2 Vols.

Basler, Roy Prentice, *Abraham Lincoln, His Speeches and Writings,* (Cleveland and New York: World Publishing Company, 1946).

Bowman, George Ernest. *The Mayflower Compact and Its Signers* (Boston, Mass.: Massachusetts Society of Mayflower Descendants, Nov. 20, 1920).

Brown, Glenn, *History of the United States Capitol,* (Washington: United States Government Printing Office, 1900-1903).

Brynestad, Lawrence E., *The Great Awakening in the New England and Middle Colonies,* (Philadelphia: Journal of the Presbyterian Historical Society. Vol. 14, No. 2, June, 1930; No. 3, September, 1930).

Caemmerer, H. P., *Washington, The National Capital,* (Washington: United States Government Printing Office).

Cotton, John, *God's Promises to His Plantations,* (London: Old South Leaflets, Twelfth Series, 1630; Boston: Old South Meeting House, 1894).

Documents Illustrative of the Formation of the Union of the American States, (Washington: United States Government Printing Office).

Foote, Henry W., *Thomas Jefferson, Champion of Religious Freedom,* (Boston: Beacon Press, 1947).

Ford, George L., *The Miracle of America.* (Grand Rapids: Zondervan Publishing House, 1963).

Hall, Thomas C., *Religious Background of American Culture.* (Boston: Little, Brown and Company, 1930).

Hall, Verna M., *Christian History of the Constitution of the United States of America,* (California: The American Constitution Press, 1961. 2 Vols.).

Hill, John Wesley, *Abraham Lincoln, Man of God,* (New York and London: G. P. Putnam's Sons, 1930).

Huszar, George B., and Henry W. Littlefield, *Basic American Documents,* (Paterson, New Jersey: Littlefield, Adams & Co., 1956).

Inaugural Addresses of the Presidents of the United States. From George Washington, 1789, to John F. Kennedy, 1961, (Washington: United States Government Printing Office).

Jefferson, Thomas, *The Life and Morals of Jesus of Nazareth,* (Boston: Beacon Press, 1961).

Thomas Jefferson National Memorial, National Park Service Publication, (Washington: United States Government Printing Office).

Johnson, Edward, *Wonder-Working Providence of Sion's Saviour in New England,* (Andover, Massachusetts: Warren F. Draper, 1867).

Johnston, William Dawson, *History of the Library of Congress,* Vol. I, 1800-1864. Washington: United States Government Printing Office, 1904).

Johnstone, William J., *Abraham Lincoln, The Christian,* (New York: Abingdon Press, 1928).

Jones, Rufus M. and others, *The Quakers in the American Colonies,* (New York: Macmillan, 1911).

Lincoln Memorial, National Park Service Publication, (Washington: United States Government Printing Office).

Kane, Joseph Nathan, *Facts About the Presidents,* (New York: The H. W. Wilson Company, 1959).

Mathews, James McFarlane, *The Bible and Civil Government,* (New York: Robert Carter and Brothers, 1838).

Miller, Perry, and Thomas M. Johnson, *The Puritans,* (New York: American Book Company, 1938).

Nuttall, Geoffrey F., *The Holy Spirit in Puritan Faith and Experience,* (Oxford: Basil Blackwell, 1946).

Our Capital, Senate Document No. 22, (Washington: United States Government Printing Office).

Rossiter, Clinton Lawrence, *Seedtime of the Republic,* (New York: Harcourt, Brace, and Company, 1953).

Sachse, Julius Friedrich, *The German Pietists of Provincial Pennsylvania,* (Philadelphia: printed for the author, 1895).

Stephenson, George Malcom, *The Puritan Heritage.* (New York: Macmillan, 1952).

The Supreme Court of the United States, (Washington: United States Government Printing Office, 1946).

Sweet, William W., *The Story of Religion in America,* (New York: Harper and Brothers, 1930).

———— *Religion in Colonial America,* (New York: Charles Scribner's Sons, 1949).

Thomas, Elbert Duncan, *This Nation Under God,* (New York: Harper and Brothers, 1950).

Umbreit, Kenneth Bernard, *Founding Fathers,* (New York: Harper and Brothers, 1941).

Viles, Jonas, *Letters and Addresses of George Washington,* (New York: Unit Book Publishing Company, 1908).

Vrooman, Lee, *The Faith that Built America,* (New York: Arrowhead Books, Inc.).

Washington Monument, National Park Service Publication, (Washington: United States Government Printing Office).

INDEX